Project Managing E-Learning

Managing an e-learning project requires more than the usual project management know-how. It requires skills of project management, instructional design, program leadership, team management, and information technology – in other words someone who can integrate two divergent fields of knowledge and make them work together seamlessly. This unique survival guide is packed with project management methods and techniques built on using a well-known systematic approach to instructional design.

Avoiding theory and focusing on valuable and practical information, *Project Managing E-Learning* integrates proven instructional design and project management techniques into one seamless process to help you successfully manage every aspect of the e-learning development cycle, from cost estimate to product delivery.

Highlighting the most common development problems and how to avoid them, this book will teach you how to:

- organize the project;
- establish the scope;
- calculate costs and risks;
- design the work breakdown structure;
- prepare estimates and proposals for contracts;
- manage teams for maximum quality and productivity.

Full of expert advice guidelines, and templates, *Project Managing E-Learning* will help you to bring your e-learning project in on schedule, within budget, and to your clients' satisfaction. It is essential reading for those in higher education institutions, as well as those in corporations and corporate universities involved in employee and customer training online. It will also appeal to educational administrators and students in Education, Business Management, MIS, or Instructional Technology Programs.

Maggie McVay Lynch is Director of Teaching and Learning Services at Oregon Health and Sciences University, Oregon, USA.

John Roecker is Career Framework Manager at the Project Management Institute, Pennsylvania, USA.

D1425578

Project Managing E-Learning

A handbook for successful design, delivery and management

Maggie McVay Lynch and
John Roecker

Routledge
Taylor & Francis Group

LONDON AND NEW YORK

First published 2007
by Routledge
2 Park Square, Milton Park, Abingdon, Oxon OX14 4RN

Simultaneously published in the USA and Canada
by Routledge
270 Madison Ave, New York, NY 10016

Routledge is an imprint of the Taylor & Francis Group, an informa business

Typeset in Sabon by
RefineCatch Limited, Bungay, Suffolk
Printed and bound in Great Britain by
MPG Books Ltd, Bodmin

British Library Cataloguing in Publication Data
A catalogue record for this book is available from the British Library

Library of Congress Cataloging-in-Publication Data
Lynch, Maggie McVay, 1954–
   Project managing e-learning : a handbook for successful design,
delivery and management / Maggie McVay Lynch and John Roecker.
      p. cm.
   Includes bibliographical references and index.
   1. Project management. 2. Web-based instruction—Management.
3. Internet in education. I. Roecker, John, 1942– II. Title.
   HD69.P75L96 2007
   658.3′12402854678—dc22
   2006039511

ISBN10: 0–415–77219–2 (hbk)
ISBN10: 0–415–77220–6 (pbk)
ISBN10: 0–203–94699–5 (ebk)

ISBN13: 978–0–415–77219–8 (hbk)
ISBN13: 978–0–415–77220–4 (pbk)
ISBN13: 978–0–203–94699–2 (ebk)

For Jim, whose continued support of my career and writing is invaluable to managing my time and commitments

For Barbara, whose support of my dreams enables me to realize them

Contents

Figures

Tables

Acknowledgements

No book of this scope is written without help. First, we are thankful for the community of e-learning faculty, administrators, and students who have freely shared their experiences and sometimes research and case studies that were years in the making. In particular, we are grateful to the following researchers who gave permission to use their work:

- Joseph Clark at Florida State University for his course templates;
- Bryan Bauer, Dave Carson, Paula Yalpani, and Gail Wortman at Iowa Learning Online, partnered with Iowa Public Television, for their Anatomy and Physiology Course example;
- Coley O'Brien, Director of Sears Merchandise Training, for his Complex ELMS Diagnostic Spreadsheet;
- Misty Hamideh, Instructional Designer and Adjunct Faculty member, Portland State University, for her icon-driven navigation in the first-year Spanish course, Como; and
- Virgil Varvel, University of Illinois for his metaphorical template.

Finally, special thanks goes to Dennis Gilbert at Portland State University. Through countless meetings and discussions about this book and his participation in a variety of e-learning projects, he provided a great example of how to evaluate risks and constraints. His ability to think clearly, plan ahead, and stay calm in the face of pending disaster is certainly something to be emulated. A veteran of planning and managing a variety of IT projects with limited budgets, very tight timelines, and often difficult political circumstances, Dennis has been a great friend and mentor in how to effectively meld IT and learning.

How to use this book

To give you a head start in developing your e-learning project management process documents, this book includes a companion website located at http://www.routledge.com/textbooks/9780415772204 where all the template forms are located. Anytime we discuss a form or document to be used in developing and managing your e-learning system, you have the opportunity to download the template from this website. You may wish to download the documents in advance and have them ready to populate as you work through the processes we discuss.

This book is based on two models, the ADDIE model for course development and the IPECC model for project management. Both of these models are iterative processes. You do not progress in a straight line. Instead you often must return to a previous process in the model before you move forward. The same might be said for this book.

How is the book structured?

Following the definition of e-learning, the core processes of project management are presented in the five subsequent chapters. Each chapter will begin with an image showing the ADDIE model and the IPECC model. We hope that this will assist you in tracking the two models together.

Chapters 7 and 8 provide more in-depth discussion of two key areas of project management: quality management and change management. Though all five areas of the IPECC model are important, these two areas are key throughout the processes. Furthermore, quality and change management are so complex in themselves that entire books have been written on each. We felt that to even introduce these important concepts, we needed to devote a chapter to them.

Chapter 10 is our attempt to look into the crystal ball and make some predictions about e-learning trends. As with all predictions, some may come true and others may not. The entire project management process is about predicting what may happen as the project progresses. Before a project management plan is even begun, an organization tries to predict what the future may bring and then plan to address it before it creates problems. We hope that at least some of our predictions will provide good discussion points for you and your organization as you plan to scale your e-learning environment for the future.

How does your role change the way you use this book?

If you are new to project management, but completely familiar with the instructional design process, then you may wish to go directly to the five core processes of the IPECC model and study those. Frequently, those tasked with e-learning project management are members of a training staff in the corporate environment or a center for academic excellence and instructional design in a university environment. Whether your job is managing a team of designers or you are the sole e-learning developer in your organization, often the projects are taken one course at a time. Eventually, however, the time comes when the institution decides they want many courses developed in a short time period. This is where project management is needed.

Whether you are familiar with the ADDIE model or some other instructional design model, you will need to find the matches between your project management process and your instructional design process. Like any project manager, you must complete your projects within limited budgets and tight schedules. Yet, good instructional design principles often collide with these constraints. This book may help you to walk that tightrope between your natural good design conscience and the needs of the project when developing many courses over a short period of time.

If your background is in project management, you are probably already very familiar with the IPECC model. In that case, we suggest you pay special attention to the ADDIE model descriptions and the specific application of IPECC to the e-learning environment. Frequently, project managers in computer software or information technology departments may be tapped to be the project manager in a scaled-up e-learning environment. If this fits you, you already have a good understanding of hardware and software needs, and some facility with managing development in a software environment. However, managing non-technical people involved with instruction is probably not your forte.

Most e-learning project teams consist of content experts and/or instructors who may have very little understanding of computer processes or software design. Furthermore, they are very passionate about what is appropriate for learning design and need to have a means for translating that to the web. You may also be working with instructional designers, students, and administrators who have limited knowledge of the information technology environment they must encounter in this project.

We hope that the chapters on planning, change management, and quality management will be particularly useful to you in navigating the sea of concerns and issues that will arise between informational technology needs and instructional design needs.

Whether your role is primarily as an administrator, a project manager, an instructional designer, or a teacher, we hope this book will serve as a reference tool and help guide as you build your skills. E-learning is a vast subject, as is project management. No one book can cover all of the necessary information needed to become expert in either of these areas. Our hope is to provide an overview of both fields and how they work together, so that you could take the next step in building your e-learning environment and planning for it to scale to meet the needs of your students and instructors for many years to come.

Case studies

The case studies in this book are used to illustrate where project management might have been improved. No project goes according to plan. All projects have problems, some more than others. If your e-learning project has many problems it may cause long delays, will likely cost more money, and may end in cancellation.

All the case studies presented in these chapters come from the authors' experience in their institutions or in consulting around the world. Some of them are presented as compilations in order to make an example of a failed process. No identifying names or locations have been provided because most institutions do not wish the world to know about the mistakes they made. Our hope is that by reading the case studies, you will learn from those mistakes and at least find new ones for yourself.

What this book is not about

This book is not about project management in general. Though we use the well-known IPECC model, we have made suggestions about processes and forms that are specific to e-learning. We do not attempt to generalize our suggestions to any projects outside of e-learning and instructional design.

This book is not about managing staff, managing an instructional design department, or managing an e-learning helpdesk or resource center. Though we talk about managing people, we are specific to managing members of the project management team. These members may or may not also be part of the department you manage. Furthermore, these members may be transient – brought together for short periods of time as they are needed in specific parts of the project. Other books speak to general management and supervision principles or organizational structuring and management.

This book is not about how to design e-learning modules, courses, or curricula. Though we discuss key areas of the design process and make suggestions about what may be considered a quality module or course, we do not endeavor to provide instructional design guidelines. Again, other books are written specifically on that topic – including books by the authors.

Other books you may find useful

As we've indicated above, both e-learning and project management are large fields of knowledge. Below are other books you may find useful as a supplement to this one.

Jochems, Wim, Koper, Rob and Van Merrienboer, Jeroen (eds.) (2003). *Integrated E-Learning: Implications for Pedagogy, Technology and Organization.* RoutledgeFalmer.

McVay Lynch, Maggie (2002). *The Online Educator: A Guide to Creating the Virtual Classroom.* RoutledgeFalmer.

McVay Lynch, Maggie (2004). *Learning Online: A Guide to Success in the Virtual Classroom.* RoutledgeFalmer.

Panda, Santosh (2003). *Planning and Management in Distance Education.* RoutledgeFalmer.

Project Management Institute (2004). *A Guide to the Project Management Body of Knowledge.* PMBOK® Guide. 3rd edition.

Salmon, Gilly (2002). *E-tivities: The Key to Active Online Learning.* RoutledgeFalmer.

Chapter 1

Definition and goals of the e-learning environment

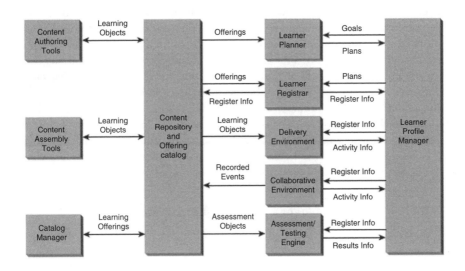

What is e-learning?

E-learning is a term that is inextricably linked to the Internet. For more than 100 years educators have had many opportunities for providing learning at a distance. It began with itinerant teachers who would travel from town to town, then correspondence courses, and eventually video tapes and CDs or DVDs were sent by mail to the learner's home. In the last 30 years synchronous training was made available through point-to-point video and eventually two-way interactive video courses. All of these have informed our practice of distance delivery and served as stepping stones to e-learning.

The primary precursor to the term e-learning was computer-based training. In fact, some would argue that because it was electronic it could be classified as e-learning. Computer-based training was set on a platform of linear instruction. Though some interaction was programmed into the course structure, the interaction moved you only in one direction. It wasn't until the collaborative aspects of learning were included in an electronic medium that e-learning came into its own.

Most researchers would agree that the term e-learning refers to that part of distance learning relying on Web-based delivery systems. To add to that definition, we would suggest that e-learning also goes beyond the mere delivery of static content. Instead it includes collaboration, both synchronous and asynchronous, as well as some type of shared learning experience with fellow students.

One of the most comprehensive definitions of e-learning was offered by William Horton (2001): "E-learning is the use of Web and Internet technologies to create experiences that educate our fellow human beings." To expand on this definition and provide details, we would add that e-learning is facilitated and supported through the use of information and communications technology, e-learning can cover a spectrum of activities from supported learning, to blended learning (the combination of traditional and e-learning practices), to learning that is entirely online. Whatever the technology, however, learning is the vital element. The wide adoption of the Internet and its social collaboration capabilities has helped e-learning to gain momentum as more people become learners and expect to use the facilities of the Web as an integral part of their learning process. Like the Web itself, the potential for e-learning seems to be growing and changing as new tools and processes become available.

Is there a specific pedagogical practice associated with e-learning?

Some would argue that the Web is primarily used as a means for wide distribution of content. Others would advocate for using the collaborative tools of the Web to enhance learning. We would suggest that pedagogy is determined by the instructional designer and/or instructor and related specifically to the topic needs and required outcomes. The use of a delivery mechanism, such as the Web, should not define a pedagogical practice. It should, instead, provide a mechanism for implementing the best pedagogy for that course or topic.

Whatever pedagogical philosophy you select, it is important to also remember that replicating something that exists within the traditional classroom is rarely the best solution for learners or teachers. Initial forays into e-learning tend to be pure content dissemination. The new e-learning developer looks at a class that was taught in lecture and then delivers that lecture over the Web, either by writing instructor notes and making them available or by physically taping the lecture and making it available. Though there may be good reason to do this in certain contexts, in most cases this is not a viable learning mechanism on its own. In fact, one might ask if the teaching strategy of a lecture in the classroom is delivering the best learning environment or just doing what has always been done. No matter what the reason for the classroom selection, on the Web the translation of that is even less effective because of the lack of physicality and certainly the lack of interaction.

It is because of this that e-learning journals, conferences, and practitioners have consistently advocated the increased use of collaborative learning tools and the decreased use of content dissemination in e-learning contexts.

What is project management?

Almost any human activity that involves carrying out a non-repetitive task can be a project. Building a backyard shed, planting a garden, planning a wedding, building a house, creating a new vehicle, launching a mission in space, building a skyscraper, creating a new drug, and developing a new computer application are all projects. So we are all project managers! We all practice project management (PM). But there is a big difference between carrying out a very simple project involving one or two people and one involving a complex mix of people, organizations, and tasks.

The art of planning for the future has always been a human trait. In essence a project can be captured on paper with a few simple elements: a start date, an end date, the tasks that have to be carried out and when they should be finished, and some idea of the resources (people, machines, etc.) that will be needed during the course of the project.

When the plan starts to involve different things happening at different times, some of which are dependent on each other, plus resources required at different times and in different quantities and perhaps working at different rates, the paper plan could start to cover a vast area and be unreadable.

Using ADDIE for design and project management

Good instructional design (ISD) and good project management is not the same thing. They may go hand in hand, but they are not interchangeable. Though we will use the familiar ADDIE model (Analyze, Design, Develop, Implement, and Evaluate) to help describe the instructional design tasks that might occur in each stage of e-learning project management, we also need to clearly state that ADDIE was never intended as a model for project management.

Figure 1.1 visually represents the ADDIE model and what occurs in each stage, as well as the relationship of the ADDIE stages to the phases of the IPECC project management model.

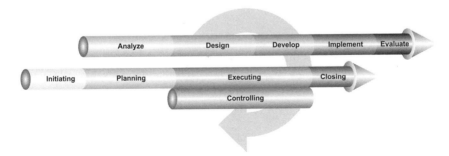

Figure 1.1 ADDIE model relationship to project management model.

The five stages of the ADDIE model are preceded by the ***initiating*** phase of our project management model. This initiating phase builds the business case for the project, determines the rough costs associated with undertaking the project and the expected organizational benefits resulting from it. This forms the overarching rationale for proceeding with the project. A project definition that outlines basic project parameters such as objectives, scope, milestones, and resource requirements is then drawn up by the project sponsor and the project manager to hand over to the project team.

Leading in to the five stages of the ADDIE model, the outputs and activities associated with each stage that need to be included in the project plan are as follows:

Analyze stage:

- Clarify organizational and training program objectives.
- Agree to the scope of the training program.
- Articulate training administration requirements.
- Determine strategies for transferring learned skills to the workplace.
- Detail project risks, opportunities, and assumptions.
- Investigate constraints in implementing the program, including technological, budget, timing, and duration.
- List training vendor/trainer selection criteria.
- Determine the target participants, program entry requirements, participant characteristics, and special needs.
- Determine extent of training participant knowledge/skill assessment required.
- Determine the tasks currently performed by target participants and level of performance required following the training.
- Estimate program design, development, implementation and evaluation costs, effort required, and schedule.

Deliverable

Training needs analysis

Design stage:

- Translate the program objectives into terminal and enabling learning objectives.
- Quantify program development, implementation and evaluation costs, and effort required.
- Determine program structure and sequence.
- Determine program duration and pace.
- Decide program format and mode of delivery.

- Specify type of participant assessments and assessment conditions.
- Determine program evaluation methodology, data collection methods, timing and reporting formats.
- Articulate transfer of learning methods and workplace support.
- Define implementation and training administration requirements.

Deliverable

High-level instructional design

Development stage:

- Develop communication packs for program stakeholders.
- Develop session plans, trainer guides, learner guides, and trainer and participant resources.
- Develop trainer and on-the-job aids.
- Develop coaching/mentoring guides and resources.
- Develop technology infrastructure and software.
- Develop participant assessments.
- Develop project and program evaluation instruments.
- Conduct pilot program to test that program meets client requirements.
- Review implementation and evaluation costs, effort required, and schedule.

Deliverables

Communication packs
Session plans
Instructor guides
Student learning guides and resources
Just-in-time training/learning aids
Participant assessment instruments
Program evaluation instruments
Project evaluation instruments

Implementation stage:

- Rollout program communications to stakeholders.
- Produce program materials and aids.
- Install technology infrastructure and services.
- Set up administrative databases and systems.
- Install on-the-job aids.
- Prepare coaches/mentors.
- Book venue, accommodation, and travel arrangements.
- Set up venue and accommodation.

- Schedule participants.
- Conduct training sessions.
- Implement training transfer strategies.
- Conduct participant assessments.
- Collect participant feedback.

Deliverables

Completed participant assessments
Completed attendance forms
Completed participant feedback forms

Evaluation stage:

- Collect training program evaluation data.
- Collect project evaluation data.
- Review training program performance (number of employees trained, percent participants passed, participant satisfaction).
- Review project performance (cost, schedule, scope, stakeholder satisfaction, project team satisfaction).
- Report program and project performance results.

Deliverables

Program evaluation report
Project evaluation report

The activities and deliverables listed above are indicative only. Each organization and each project will have its own specific requirements, so you will need to customize the list above to suit your own project's particular circumstances.

Note also that a number of project variables are more clearly articulated and calculated as the project progresses through each phase. These variables include cost, schedule, requirements, and risks, and as each of these is made more fully known, a go/no-go decision must be made at the end of each phase.

The defining project parameters remain fixed. These are project objectives, scope, deliverables, and approach. When these vary throughout the project, it is a sign that insufficient effort was put into defining the project at the outset and is an indication the proposed benefits may not eventuate.

The stages of the ADDIE model are also iterative. The feedback resulting from the evaluation stage is fed back into the next project. In this way, each successive project may improve in its delivery of expected organizational benefits.

Overview of the project management model

There are many project management models. However, for the purposes of this book, we have chosen to use the most popular model – IPECC – which is accepted worldwide in projects of all types and sizes. Hundreds of thousands of project managers are certified and trained in its use.

The IPECC model has five phases:

1 *Initiating* – Articulate your vision for the project, establish goals, and define expectations and the scope of your project.
2 *Planning* – Refine the scope, assemble your team, identify specific tasks and activities to be completed, and develop a project plan, schedule, and budget.
3 *Executing* – Accomplish your goals by developing and leading your team, solving problems, and building your project.
4 *Controlling* – Monitor changes to the project, make corrections, adjust your schedule to respond to problems, or adjust your expectations and goals.
5 *Closing* – Deliver your project to your audience, acknowledge results, and assess its success. Take the time to compose a written evaluation of the project and the development effort.

The middle three phases are not sequential. Instead they are iterative. You will find that you are constantly planning, executing, and controlling your project as necessary.

What differentiates e-learning projects from other project plans?

E-learning projects are usually significantly smaller than most project planning books describe. E-learning projects also tend to demand rapid deployment with high quality outcomes and little budget. As e-learning comes out of training divisions of corporations (usually not well-funded) or as an additional offering in educational institutions (again not well-funded), it is unique in that the expectations for success are high and the sponsorship maintains a high profile without a lot of financial backing.

E-learning projects normally don't have the luxury of lengthy needs assessments and requirements definition. In this book we will discuss the importance of needs assessment and requirements definition, but we also realize that most institutions find this stage to take too long. The challenge of your e-learning project is to find a way to keep the quality of that planning phase while still moving the project along quickly.

The products of e-learning require flexible content and learner-friendly interface designs. Most project management books and plans have much more defined end-products. Teaching and learning, however, require flexibility and tend to vary from one implementation to the next. This makes the development cycle more complex. One way of dealing with this problem is by early development of working prototypes, not just models to be discarded and replaced with the "real thing" later.

Finally, e-learning projects tend to be iterative, rather than linear, with an eye to incremental and constant change in the development lifecycle. Each cycle gets you closer to a completed product, while at the same time allowing you to demonstrate real working "builds" of your product so that your e-learning customers experience the product several times before it is completed. Their experience and feedback provides you with many opportunities to re-evaluate and assign new priorities to product features along the way.

For any e-learning project management model to work, it requires a high degree of trust between e-learning customers and the product developers, a firm grasp of risk management, great negotiating skills, and an ability to manage multiple activities within very tight timeframes. Though all projects need a project manager to do these things, an e-learning project requires one that can embrace constant change and yet stay within budget and on time.

Top 20 reasons e-learning projects fail

1   Failure to gain long-term, on-going support from management.
2   Failure to set forth an e-learning strategy that takes into account the most pressing business needs.
3   Failure to create an organizational context for producing e-learning.
4   Failure to recognize that e-learning, like most other Web-based initiatives, will require adaptive, incremental processes.
5   Failure to perform meaningful reviews of e-learning development at the end of each project to assure continuous process improvement for subsequent e-learning projects.
6   Failure to view e-learning modules as dynamic entities that will require ongoing maintenance to stay current.
7   Failure to manage risks.
8   Failure to think outside the box and use the delivery method as a prime criterion for new design, instead creating e-learning courses that merely imitate (often poorly) traditional classroom offerings.
9   Failure to distinguish between technology dazzle and real learning value.
10   Failure to build modularity and reusability into e-learning courses.
11   Failure to establish a change management strategy.
12   Failure to keep all customers/stakeholders involved and aligned with the e-learning goals of the organization.
13   Failure to dedicate full-time support to the e-learning initiative.
14   Failure to plan for the physical architecture required to support e-learning.

15   Failure to understand and/or integrate multimedia effectively in the product. Being "held hostage" by multimedia stars.

16   Failure to standardize at the risk of individual creativity, allowing instructional designers and website developers to so completely dominate the project that schedules slip and standardization is not possible.

17   Failure to recognize that e-learning, like most other Web-based initiatives, requires adaptive, incremental processes.

18   Failure to create an organizational context with clearly delineated roles and responsibilities for the e-learning development team and the other stakeholders in the e-learning project.

19   Failure to set forth an e-learning strategy that takes into account the most pressing business needs of your organization.

20   Failure to communicate plans, progress, successes, and failures among the many stakeholders in the project.

The goal of this book is to give you enough information and examples so that your project will not fall into the pitfalls that cause it to fail.

Chapter 2

Initiating the project

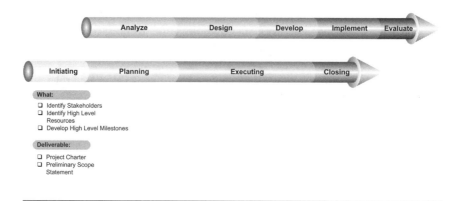

Analyze | Design | Develop | Implement | Evaluate

Initiating | Planning | Executing | Closing

What:
- ❑ Identify Stakeholders
- ❑ Identify High Level Resources
- ❑ Develop High Level Milestones

Deliverable:
- ❑ Project Charter
- ❑ Preliminary Scope Statement

During the initiating phase of the project, data is gathered to support the business case for the e-learning course and general boundaries are identified and documented in the project charter. This chapter focuses on forming a small project team to create the project charter, gather foundation data for the project charter (or business case for the course) and document the results of that research in the project charter. The illustration above outlines what the project charter team will do during the initiating phase and the deliverables from this phase.

An introduction to project teams

Projects are usually implemented by a team of people with varying roles and responsibilities. Typical roles in a project team are detailed in Table 2.1.

Each role may be performed by individuals or, alternatively, one person may function in multiple roles. In small organizations it is not unusual for an e-learning course developer to perform the roles of subject matter expert, project manager, and sponsor.

The size and membership of the project team varies for each project and as the project passes from one project phase to the next. Some roles are required for the entire duration of the project. An example of this is the project manager and the executive sponsor. Other roles are not required for the entire project – just for one phase of it. An example of this is the instructional designer who is required for the analyze and design stages of ADDIE and the planning and executing phases of IPECC. For the initiating phase of a project, a small project team is convened. Required roles for this team are the executive sponsor to outline the business need for the course, the project manager to develop the project charter and someone with a financial background, acting in the role of a

Table 2.1 Typical project team roles and responsibilities

Sponsor	• Authorizes the project. • Provides executive authority to the project team. • Helps set course goal. • Helps identify constraints. • Inspires the team.
Project Manager	• Responsible for achieving the project's deliverables. • Produces plan of action. • Monitors progress to keep the project on track. • Leads the project team. • Communicates project status/information.
Stakeholder	• Interested in or affected by project. • Contributes to the project by providing feedback.
Subject Matter Expert	• Expert in an area or profession (full-/part-time member). • Responsible for completing activities in the project plan related to their subject matter expertise (e.g., financial, instructional design, instructional development, technology, etc.).
Customer	• Internal/external person for whom the course is developed. • Influences the course.
Supplier	• Provides material, products, or services needed for the course design, development, or implementation. • Delivers supplies on time and provides services or goods at the agreed cost (as agreed by the project manager at the outset of the project).

subject matter expert, to complete the financial resources section of the project charter.

When identifying project team members, it is important to ensure that you do not overlook subject matter experts from organizations that might not be required for instructor-led courses. One of these organizations is the information technology department, or an educational communications department. E-learning courses may have additional infrastructure requirements including discussion forums, chat rooms, audio/video conferencing, etc. The information technology department may either specify required technologies and/or control them. Additionally, the course may require access to data sources which other departments control. Thus, it is wise to include members from these departments as part of the project team.

Depending on the organizational structure, securing team member participation may be a significant concern. In a functional or hierarchal organization, in which the employee has one clear superior who sets the employee's goals and grants pay increases, support for the project and the project manager may be limited by the team member's superior. The superior's lack of acceptance for the project, or benign neglect of its importance, may present a resource constraint to the project manager, e.g., the superior will not allow or empower the project team member to participate effectively. In this instance, executive sponsorship is of extreme importance as they may be able to negotiate with the project team member's superior on your behalf.

The project manager

The role that is the focus of this book, and the individual who is ultimately responsible for managing the project, is the project manager. The role of the project manager is to execute the project plan, to communicate the status of the project to stakeholders, and to develop the project team. The project manager does not need to be an expert in course design and development, in the instance of this project. It is important for the project manager to have enough knowledge of course design and development to be able to communicate with project team members and to ensure that the team is not being "led astray" – but the project manager does not need to be the instructional design or development subject matter expert. Similarly, project team members should have cursory knowledge of the project management process to be able to communicate with the project manager – they must be able to understand project management terms and processes. In addition to identifying key project team members and the project sponsor, the project manager and/or the initial project team must consider data requirements for the course.

Requisite skills for project managers are, in addition to project management skills, interpersonal and leadership skills. Project management is composed of several different types of activities such as:

1 planning the work or objectives;
2 assessing and mitigating risk;
3 estimating resources;
4 allocation of resources;
5 organizing the work;
6 acquiring human and material resources;
7 assigning tasks;
8 directing activities;
9 controlling project execution;
10 tracking and reporting progress; and
11 analyzing the results based on the facts achieved.

In some organizations, typically large organizations with mature project management processes, the roles of assessing and mitigating risk, estimating resources, and developing the project schedule may be handled by a risk management specialist, an estimating specialist, or a scheduling specialist. However, in most instances, these activities are performed by the project manager. Certainly, project managers oversee all of these activities.

The executive sponsor

The role of the executive sponsor is to shepherd the project through the organization throughout its lifecycle. Most importantly, the executive sponsor must foster a culture of communication, direction, teamwork, and excitement among the many groups that must work together to ensure the project is a success.

The executive sponsor must also have enough power to direct department managers to free up team members for the project, at least on a part-time basis, for the duration of the project. Most people are overworked in the best of circumstances, and it is easy for them to put aside your project for more urgent, immediate tasks. The executive sponsor can alleviate confusion over project priorities, however, by continually supporting the project and monitoring the performance of team members.

Many techniques to gain executive sponsorship for the project exist. The following incomplete list identifies some of these techniques:

1   Identifying an organizational objective that is met by the course. An example of this is the development of a new course that trains users on a new sales technique with a new bonus program for salespersons. An indirect outcome of the course is higher sales and profits resulting from salespersons applying the new sales technique.
2   Identifying an executive's business objective that is met by the course. An example of this is the development of a new course that trains users on the use of a new product. An outcome of the new product and the course is an increase in customer satisfaction – an organizational objective. Alerting the executive sponsor to this may secure their support for the project.
3   Identifying an objective of an employee who has influence over a potential executive sponsor. Many individuals are very influential in the organization but are not highly positioned within the organization – they are hidden influencers. Your task is twofold:

    i   to convince the influencer that your project is significant; and
    ii   to identify a goal of the influencer for which you may have some control.

The stakeholder

Stakeholders are anyone who is affected by the development of the course. As such, this is a very broad group of people. Examples of this are the project team members, the executive sponsor, the project manager, end users of the course, customer service personnel, and members of the school board. The role of the stakeholder is to provide feedback on any aspect of the design, development, or implementation of the course.

The subject matter experts (SMEs)

Subject matter experts are experts in their area or profession. Their role on the project team is to provide guidance to the team on their field of expertise. Examples of SMEs are a faculty member or tutor, an engineer from the new product development team, a person from the finance department, someone from the customer service team, an instructional designer, an instructional developer, a programmer, and a member of the research department. The size of the project team varies based on the needs of the project phase and the needs of the project team. SMEs move into and out of the team when their expertise is required.

The customer

Customers are those who will use the course. They may be internal or external to the corporation or educational institution. When the course is being designed and developed, the role of the customer is to be actively involved in the project to help ensure its successful completion. Customers might be used to ensure that:

- course navigation is intuitive;
- the language used in the course is clear;
- the course may be operated on their equipment;
- the course will operate in their geographic area.

The supplier

The role of the supplier is to provide material, products, or services needed for course design, development, or implementation. Suppliers may play a significant role in enhancing competitive advantage by truly becoming a member of the organization or project team. Many organizations create long-term relationships with select suppliers. This aids the organization by eliminating the need to indoctrinate the supplier on the purpose of the organization, its operating principles and procedures, and objectives of key members of the organization. The desire for this tight relationship with a supplier must be offset with organizational requirements of due diligence and objectivity.

Build the business case – the project charter

A project charter is your business case; your reason for getting the project done. It is meant to focus on *what* you want to do and *why* you think it needs to be done. For smaller projects, your project charter should also have detail about *how* you plan to implement your project. Since you're not writing a project plan, the charter must be comprehensive. For larger projects, you need to write a project plan. Planning a project takes time, and therefore resources, so the charter is designed for you to get approval to spend this time and use these resources to write your plan.

The business case for your course or program is based on analysis of the data collected regarding reasons for the project and input from the project sponsor. When the project sponsor and project manager agree to and approve the business case, as documented in the project charter, the project manager has the authority to proceed with the project. Since the project charter provides the foundation for the entire project, the project manager should ensure that it is as comprehensive as possible.

It should also be understood that not everything will be known at the beginning of the project; consequently, a change management process will be required in the subsequent phases of the project. An example of this is the cost estimate. In the initiating phase of the project, the cost estimate is most likely a not-to-exceed estimate. That estimate will be refined further in the planning phase, Chapter 3, using a different process. As the project is executed, the cost of the project will change as requests for change are approved.

Now – back to the project charter. The project charter is typically a document of from 5–10 pages long (illustrated in Figure 2.1). The format for your project charter may differ from the illustration depending on the needs of your organization, the formality of decision-making and sign-off, and the size of your project. On a large e-learning project, such as the migration of courses from one learning management system to another, the project charter may be 10–20 pages long as this type of project will require a great deal of money and resources over a long period of time. On small projects, such as the development of a single course or group of courses for a certificate program, the project charter may only be 2–3 pages and used more as a form of agreement between a few people.

On small projects, your project charter may be classified better as a "team charter." Typically, team charters include such deliverables as a business case, problem and goal statements, scope, milestones, and roles. What should be added, perhaps in the team charter, or as a separate deliverable, is a plan or strategy for communicating information that is related to the project.

At a minimum, this communication strategy should outline how the proceedings of team meetings and project work will be communicated so that others in the organization who are on a need-to-know basis will be assured that they remain in the loop. A simple table could be constructed that would display what will be communicated, who will do the communicating, when the communication will take place, to whom the communication will be delivered, how the communications will be delivered, and where the information will be stored:

- **who** – person who is responsible for delivering the communication, e.g., project manager, instructional designer, team member;

Project Charter

Project Title: [Click **here** and type name]
Project Manager: [Click **here** and type name]

Description
Project need: [Click **here** and briefly describe the reason for the project]
Project description:
[Click **here** and briefly describe the project (preliminary project scope statement]
Project Start Date: [Click **here** and type date]
Projected Finish Date: [Click **here** and type date]

Objective
[Click **here** and enter measurable and specific objectives accomplished by this project]

Assumptions, constraints, and risks
Assumptions: [Click **here** and summarize assumptions made in this project]
Constraints: [Click **here** and summarize the constraints of this project]
Risks: [Click **here** and outline the risks involved with this project]

Resources
Financial: [Click **here** and enter projected budget in whole currency amount]
Personnel: [Click **here** and summarize personnel required to complete this project]
Material: [Click **here** and outline materials required to complete this project]

Approach
[Click **here** and outline high-level steps and milestone dates to complete this project]

Roles and responsibilities

Name	Role	Responsibility
[Click **here** and type name]	Project Sponsor	Monitor Project
[Click **here** and type name]	Project Manager	Plan and Execute Project
[Click **here** and type name]	[Click **here** and type name]	[Click **here** and type responsibility]

Sign-off

_____

[Click **here** and type sponsor name]. [Click **here** and type sponsor title].   Date

_____

[Click **here** and type project manager name]. [Click **here** and type project manager title].   Date

Comments

Figure 2.1 Illustration of project charter.

- **what** – the type of communication, e.g., team meetings, meeting minutes, team work/action items, project status reports, project timeline, project prototypes, project success stories/storyboards;
- **why** – the rationale for the communication plan, i.e., to establish and enforce a contract for communication;
- **where** – the location where the recipient will find the communication, if specified, e.g., website address, intranet location, discussion board posting;
- **when** – the time and/or frequency at which the communication is delivered, e.g., every Friday at close of business, weekly, monthly, or quarterly reports;
- **how** – the delivery mechanism that will facilitate the communication, e.g., e-mail, voice mail, conference call, live or streamed video-conference;
- **to whom** – the audience or recipients of the communication, e.g., senior management, the quality department, project champion, team members, all faculty, all departmental staff.

Table 2.2 provides a simple table communication plan example for a single course development project. Depending on your small project, this table may be replicated for multiple courses.

By establishing this communication tool up front and verifying it with the project team, the team is made aware of the important role of communicating the team's work. The members who need information the most are often subject matter experts (instructors who are responsible for teaching the course), who may not be part of the daily work of the project team, but whose knowledge on the content and teaching strategies is valuable to the team or to the organization. These experts need to be kept in the loop as the project progresses so that, when key meetings are to ensue, they are informed and can be an active participant in the discussions when important business decisions are made. It is also important that those who will facilitate the course in the future agree to its structure and implementation. Otherwise, your course will never be taught in the form the team worked so hard to achieve. A well-conceived communication plan helps to ensure that potential contributors are not left out of the loop.

More complex projects may not require much more than a two-page description and a communication plan. The difference is that the plan may be broader when delineated in the project charter. An example of a communication plan for the learning management system (LMS) migration project described previously is provided in Table 2.3.

Complex projects may end up with a project charter that is easily ten pages, because of the additional details that are required. To assist you, Figure 2.1 (the project charter illustration) is also provided as an MS Word document template on the companion website (http://www.routledge.com/textbooks/9780415772204). You may wish to use this as the foundational document for your project charter on complex projects.

Table 2.2 Simple table communication plan for small project

What	To Whom	When	Who	How	Where
Project Team Meetings	Project Team, Invitees	Weekly (every Thurs @ 9AM)	Project Manager, Instructional Designer, Multimedia Developer, Support Staff	Notices, agendas sent out one week in advance via Web calendar	SN 411
Meeting Minutes	Distribution List	By next day COB	Support Staff	e-mail	MS Word file on shared drive
Team Work/ Action Items	Project Manager	As new items are developed	Project Manager, Instructional Designer, Multimedia Developer, Support Staff	e-mail	MS Excel file on shared drive
Status Reports, including Timeline	Project Team, Sponsor, Customer	Monthly (first business day of each month)	Project Manager	e-mail	MS Word file on shared drive, and e-mail attachment to Customer
Project Budget	Sponsor, Project Financial Analyst, Quality Dept Head	TBD	Project Manager	e-mail	MS Excel file on shared drive
Project Reviews	Project Team, Sponsor, Quality Dept Head	TBD (Monthly)	Project Manager	Notices sent out one week in advance via web calendar	SN–602
Project Storyboard and/or prototypes	Instructor(s), Curriculum Committee, Sponsor	TBD	Project Manager	Demonstration notices sent out two weeks prior	Video conference demo room

Table 2.3 Communication plan for large LMS migration project

Committee/Group	Frequency	Report Focus
Teaching and Learning Council (Steering Committee)	3–4 times/year	• General status • Risk status • Progress • Decisions
Working Reference Group	Monthly	• General status • Risk status • Progress • Decisions • Budget vs. Actual
Operational Working Group	Monthly	• Timelines • Task allocation • Progress • Reports from sub-working groups • Collaboration and information dissemination across groups
Project and Sub-Project Teams	Bi-weekly	• Timelines • Task allocation • Progress • Issues

Project charter fields and sample contents are included with the project charter template. However, the description, resources, and constraints fields are particularly important and need further explanation and illustration here. We will use the example of migrating from one learning management system to another throughout our illustrations of content in these fields.

Description fields

The description area of the project charter briefly describes the project by documenting:

- the reason the e-learning project is being undertaken (project need);
- a brief description of the project (preliminary scope statement described in more detail later in this chapter);
- the start and finish dates for the project.

The project charter is the contract between the executive sponsor and the project manager – it describes the project and defines its goal. When this project is finished, the executive sponsor and project manager will refer to the project charter to locate the agreed project goal and description to verify commitments.

Example: Description section of a project charter

Business objective and executive overview

The purpose of this project is to migrate from WebCT Standard Edition to Sakai. Migration will include resources from ITS, TEDI, Library and the assistance of the academic staff. The steering committee is designated as the Teaching and Learning Council, which includes faculty representatives from each of the schools and the project manager.

The following items are not within the scope of this project but will be scoped separately in 2007:

- development of strategies for increased uptake and usage of e-learning at the university;
- conversion of non-WebCT courses to Sakai.

Resources field

The resources area of the project charter outlines the financial, personnel, and material commitments required to complete the project tasks, such as new course development, old course migration, testing, and deployment. At this stage of the project, these resource requirements may be expressed in "not to exceed" values. The requirements are estimated with more finality and in more detail in the project management plan developed in Chapter 3. The personnel field in this resources section might identify the estimated commitment by role. An example of this for a small project is:

Instructional design	180 days – April through June
Developer	160 days – July through October
System test	120 days – November through December

For a larger project, such as our LMS migration project, this section may be significantly longer as in the example opposite.

Another way to identify the personnel resources in the initial project charter would be to identify only the actual project management team commitment as in Table 2.4. The additional personnel would then be identified later in the planning document.

Example: Initial resource estimate for project charter

Resources needed

The implementation of Sakai will require the following activities:

- allocation of a project manager;
- allocation of staff to implementation teams;
- development and implementation of a detailed project plan;
- development and implementation of a communication and change management plan;
- purchasing and installation of the software and hardware;
- provision of technical training for technical support and helpdesk staff;
- provision of training in the use of Sakai for instructional and course designers, and students;
- provision of technical training and pedagogical staff development for teaching staff, course designers, and tutors;
- Provision of Sakai-specific helpdesk service for staff and students;
- Review and development of e-learning related policies and procedures;
- integration of Sakai with the Student Information System (Banner);
- development of single sign-on for Sakai;
- development of a CSS template for Sakai;
- archiving of courses from WebCT Campus Edition;
- conversion of 10 courses to Sakai for pilot, Fall 2005;
- conversion of all existing WebCT courses to Sakai for Fall 2006;
- development of processes and procedures for the conversion of non-WebCT courses by Winter 2007.

Initial estimated budget: $800,000–$1,300,000

Identification of personnel resources outlines to the executive sponsor the organizational commitment required to complete the course. It also identifies required external organizational commitments for personnel outside of the executive sponsor's control. For example, the system test personnel above may be located in the information technology department of the organization – outside of the sphere of control of the executive sponsor. The executive sponsor may need to campaign for these resources to secure them from competing demands.

The initial estimated budget is not expected to be set in stone. However, in a complex project that will run into the hundreds of thousands, or millions, of dollars, it is necessary to place a ballpark figure at the project charter stage. You do not want to be in the position of getting sign-off on a project that has no hope of receiving the funding it needs.

Table 2.4 Project management team commitment chart

Name	Role	Phone	Commitment
Maggie Lynch	University-wide Project Manager	59035	Full time
John Roecker	IT Project Manager	53763	Initially 2 days per week, then as required
Patricia Cornman	Instructional Design Manager	56725	Initially 2 days per week, then as required

Constraints field

Project managers pay attention to all aspects of the project – but are particularly concerned about competing demands of the project, defined as the triple constraints of the project. These competing demands are alternatively defined, by various sources, as:

* time – resources – scope
* scope – time – cost
* scope – cost – schedule
* time – cost – performance.

For the purposes of this text, we define the triple constraints of a project as time, resources, and scope with the addition of quality, as illustrated in Figure 2.2.

A project manager's concern is to control the dimensions of project scope, project time, and project resources (personnel and/or material) while conforming to the quality requirements of the project. Any change in one of the dimensions causes a corresponding change in at least one other dimension. For instance, if the project sponsor, or any other stakeholder in the project, recommends a change that causes an increase in project scope, the project will either take longer (an increase in project time), require an increase in resources (personnel and/or materials), or a decrease in project quality to meet the requirements as specified in the project charter.

Figure 2.2 Triple constraints.

The project charter defines the constraints of these key parameters: the preliminary project scope and time in the description fields of the project charter and resources in the resources fields of the project charter. Since the project charter is the contract between the project sponsor and the project manager, completing these fields in as much detail as possible is of the utmost importance. An example of the constraints outlined for our LMS migration project is provided below.

Example: Initial risk and constraints estimate for project charter

Risk estimate

Risk Description	Likelihood	Impact	Risk Reduction Strategies
Courses converted into Sakai do not display or perform as expected.	Low	High	• IT and TLS are carrying out comprehensive pre-testing before conversion proceeds. • The implementation team is converting courses with sufficient time allocated for testing and correction, by IT, TLS, and academics, prior to student use. • Documentation from other universities that have engaged in a similar conversion process has been reviewed.
Systems are unstable and unable to carry Fall term loads.	Medium	High	• A staged implementation plan is being developed to minimize risk of system instability. • In collaboration with IT experts, a disaster recovery plan will be developed along with regular system health checks and maintenance schedules.
Change management is not handled appropriately.	Medium	High	• A change management and communication plan is being developed to support change management processes. • The workload of existing WebCT developers will be minimized by the efforts of the implementation team in providing all conversion and thorough testing.

- Provision of comprehensive staff development and training will allay concerns and instill confidence in the new system.
- Helpdesk and website support will provide additional guidance for users.
- The ease of use of Sakai should make the move to a new system acceptable.

Project dependencies

The planning of further related projects is happening concurrently with the Sakai implementation project, however the successful completion of this project is not dependent upon them. Their scope will include:

- the selection and implementation of a content management system;
- the conversion of non-WebCT courses to Sakai;
- the development of strategies for uptake and usage of e-learning university-wide;
- the evaluation and implementation of Sakai non-core subsystems.

Constraints

- Academic term timelines are set and must be considered for the project.
- WebCT license end dates.
- Budget is set at $950,000.

Assumptions

- That all existing WebCT courses will be successfully converted into Sakai.
- That all courses archived in WebCT will be retrievable if needed to backtrack.
- That the budget will cover all project requirements.
- That the current reporting structure will enable rather than impede progress.

Preliminary scope statement

A final output of the initiating phase of the e-learning course project is the development of the preliminary project scope statement. The preliminary project scope statement identifies:

- initial project organization
- project goal(s)
- dates of key project events
- budget and resource constraints.

Of these items, the project organization and key project events will be discussed more fully. Considering the brief information outlined above, the preliminary project scope statement is most likely one paragraph long.

The project organization area

This paragraph should outline the number of and roles of full- and part-time participants on the initial project team, the anticipated schedule of meetings (e.g., one full day meeting per week) and the need for a physical or virtual project team room.

The output of the initial project team should also be clearly understood. The project plan is an example of the output of this initial project team. The resources outlined are those required to define and develop the project plan. Since the project sponsor is securing team members on behalf of the project and project manager, this area should provide a clear understanding of the required personnel and their roles in sufficient detail to enable the project sponsor to make the case for these resources. The key project events section might identify dates for key deliverables like the project plan, course design, pilot offering, and course completion. Additional information related to the project charter and preliminary scope statement is included in the project charter template included with this text.

Initiating phase summary

The initiating phase of the project develops two key project deliverables, the project charter and a preliminary project scope statement. While the preliminary project scope statement will be refined in the next phase of the project, the planning phase, the project charter is the contract between the project sponsor and project manager and as such will not be updated in later project phases. A signed project charter, by the project sponsor, authorizes design and development of the course. During the planning phase of the project, Chapter 3 of this text, the initial project team will create the plan that will manage the analysis, design, and development of the e-learning course.

Chapter 3

Planning the project

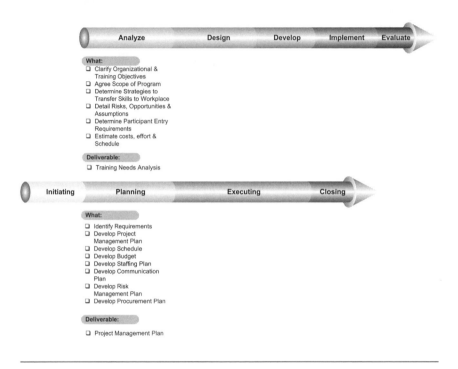

Planning is of major importance to a project because the project involves doing something which has not been done before. The planning phase of the project identifies the processes and procedures that will complete the project, ideally, on time, within budget, and with the agreed requirements. The amount of planning performed should be commensurate with the scope of the project and the usefulness of the information developed. During the planning phase of the project, the project manager plus key members of the project team use the project charter and the preliminary project scope statement, developed in the initiation phase, to develop a project management plan. The project management plan may be a sizeable document or report with multiple tabs for each relevant plan or the project plan may be brief in the form of an e-mail or memo containing only a paragraph covering each of the plans. Figure 3.1 identifies inputs to the planning process as well as suggested contents for the project management plan.

The opening graphic of this chapter outlines the actions that the project team will follow during the analyze stage of ADDIE and the planning phase of IPECC. This graphic also identifies the training needs analysis as an output

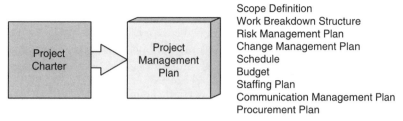

Scope Definition
Work Breakdown Structure
Risk Management Plan
Change Management Plan
Schedule
Budget
Staffing Plan
Communication Management Plan
Procurement Plan

Figure 3.1 Input to and output from the planning process.

of the analyze stage of ADDIE and the project management plan as an output of the planning phase of IPECC. However, analysis activities have been summarized in this figure. The following is a list of actions to be considered during the analysis stage of ADDIE.

- Clarify organizational and training program objectives.
- Agree to the scope of the training program.
- Articulate training administration requirements.
- Determine strategies for transferring learned skills to the workplace.
- Detail project risks, opportunities, and assumptions.
- Investigate constraints in implementing the program, including technological, budget, timing, and duration.
- List training vendor/trainer selection criteria.
- Determine the target participants, program entry requirements, participant characteristics, and special needs.
- Determine extent of training participant knowledge/skill assessment required.
- Determine the tasks currently performed by target participants and level of performance required following the training.
- Estimate program design, development, implementation and evaluation costs, effort required, and schedule.

Deliverable

Training needs analysis

Relationship of ADDIE analysis stage to project planning

If your organization has an immediate need for e-learning and a very short timeline, it is tempting to skip over the analysis stage of ADDIE and just start writing the actual training materials. By following this action, you might save production time in the short term, but will you actually save time and money in the long term? Many institutions wrestle with this question, and their decisions are all based on risk.

If you're thinking about reducing the scope of your project's needs analysis stage, here are some questions that will help you assess your level of risk:

- What might happen if you skip the ADDIE analysis stage and start creating course content?
- How will the course's quality (and results) be affected?
- How much design and development time could the institution save?
- If you discover something later and have to fix it, will it take more time or cost more in the long run?

In many ways, your choice will be an economic one. If you choose speed over quality, you want to be clear with all your stakeholders as to the expectations of the course design. If you choose quality over speed, you have problems as well in that you may not be able to deliver an entire program in the timeframe needed for students to complete degrees or certificates in a timely manner. It is always a trade-off.

Analysis and quality assurance

The ADDIE analysis stage serves as a formal planning and quality assurance process. It defines the project's objectives using the language of instructional design, and it validates that the course will meet the organization's needs and the learners' needs. If you don't perform the needs analysis, you will increase the project's risk.

In many ways, an e-learning project is very similar to a software development project. If you were leading a software project, you could start the project by asking engineers to analyze the project's needs and plan the application. However, you could also start the project by asking programmers to start writing code. If the programmers write code without a plan and a clear goal, they're likely to produce a software application that doesn't quite do what it needs to do. The code may also have a lot of bugs that may not be discovered until late in the development cycle or even post-launch.

In the software industry, one standard metric states that QA planning and review activities produce a 10:1 return on investment. It's less costly to prevent software bugs through planning than by fixing them line by line in the code. The same principle applies to e-learning projects. If you can identify mistaken assumptions during the assessment stage, it'll be easier and less expensive to correct them. If you wait until the course materials have been written, it'll be more expensive to go back and make changes.

Timeliness vs. quality

Sometimes, a company has to choose between getting the training project done (timeliness) and getting the training project right (quality). Table 3.1 illustrates some reasons why companies make their choices.

Although some institutions try to save time by skipping the needs analysis stage, they may not save time overall. Unanswered questions from the analysis stage can bring the design and development process to a complete halt later.

Some potential risks

Table 3.2 illustrates some of the risks that your organization would face if you reduce or omit the steps in the training needs analysis stage.

Project description data

Complex projects in some ways are easier to describe because there has probably been a lot of requirement identification – surveys, analysis, and executive decisions – around the need for the project. However, on small projects, such as designing a new online course or series of courses, the sponsor may be a single faculty member or a manager of distance education. These course-specific projects often skip the step of describing the project, which may end up hampering the final buy-in and distribution of the course(s).

How do you identify the need for a new e-learning course? If you work in an academic setting, does a professor request a new e-learning course? If you are

Table 3.1 Decision-making in timeliness vs. quality

Reasons to Choose Timeliness	Reasons to Choose Quality
• The project will make only slight modifications to an existing, well-written course.	• Course will be entirely new.
• The organization's business needs indicate that it's better to deliver a partial training solution on time than miss the deadline.	• Business goals are unclear or have changed.
• Course is a one-shot event for a very small group of learners.	• The e-learning program must achieve measurable results. • Course covers compliance issues or critical business processes. • Course will be used for a long period of time or delivered to a large audience. • An existing course will be rewritten for a new learning audience with different needs.

Table 3.2 Risks to omitting the ADDIE analysis stage

If You Skip This Step . . .	. . . Here Are Some Possible Risks
Discovery	• Designer/developers may not know about (or use) important information when designing the course. • Designer/developers might not talk to the right subject matter experts.
Business Goals	• The course may not be written to support the business's goals. • It may be difficult to measure the course's effectiveness or results.
Learner Analysis	• If the course content is too easy for learners, they may become bored. • If the course content is too difficult for learners, they may become frustrated.
Instructional Analysis	• The course may omit critical steps and information. • The course may become bogged down with less-important information.
Learning Objectives	• The project omits a major QA checkpoint that allows you to review and confirm the course's objectives. • Mistaken assumptions may not be caught until much later in the project. • These mistakes may be more costly to correct.

the designer, subject matter expert, and professor, do you identify the next great course and run with the idea? If you work in a corporate setting, does the director of a service or product line request a new course to market or support their new product? We'd like to suggest another method of determining the need – fact-based requirements identification.

Requirement identification is the process of identifying and documenting audience and technical constraints for the development and use of the e-learning course. How will you acquire those facts, that data? There are numerous methods to gather the initial requirements for a course. They may include surveys of prospective attendees, results from end of course feedback forms, unmet organizational business needs or requirements, etc. For an e-learning course, two categories of requirements are essential: participant and technical.

Regarding participant requirements for the course, you may need to determine prerequisite knowledge and skills – i.e., what must the attendee know and be able to do before taking this course. For example, does the course presume knowledge and skill in HTML programming, Internet page design and development, design and development of forms, etc.? Additionally, are there software applications that the participant must be able to execute?

Must they be proficient in Microsoft Word, Excel, WordPad? What is the level of skill required when using these applications? Are they beginner, intermediate, or advanced?

In some instances, the geographic location of the participant may be relevant. Examples of geographic relevance are the time zone of the participant, particularly if the e-learning course has synchronous components (e.g., chats with the instructor or other participants, conference calls with the instructor or other participants, etc.). A chat between an instructor located in the Pacific time zone of the United States and participants located in Europe, the Middle East, China, and New Zealand may require someone to be up at 3 a.m. or midnight. One way to plan for this eventuality is to schedule multiple chat sessions, sometimes at times inconvenient to the instructor, in order to limit participant inconvenience. Additionally, how do you state the time of the chat or of homework delivery deadlines? Do you say 6.00 p.m. or do you say 18.00 GMT?

In addition to geographic concerns, cultural aspects of the participants may also be relevant. Examples of cultural concerns may be lack of participation due to respect for the instructor, lack of participation due to gender (in some cultures, females will not offend males), lack of participation due to cultural differences (e.g., considerations for holidays, siesta times, evening dinner participation, etc.). All of these considerations impact student desire/need/ability to participate regularly. Another concern with delivery to multiple geographic areas and/or cultures, is the use of slang. An example of this is illustrated in Table 3.3 with the difference in terminology between two seemingly identical languages – English and American English.

Although these differences may seem inconsequential, in many instances to those in the affected culture they are far from inconsequential. The authors are aware of complaints of cultural insensitivity because magazines are printed in the United States on 8½ × 11 inch paper vs. A4 paper, or that this book uses American spellings even when printed in the UK, Australia, or Canada. These seemingly inconsequential differences, if not considered carefully, may limit the acceptance of the course by the intended participants.

Table 3.3 Differences in common terminology and slang spellings

American English	English
elevator	lift
automobile hood	bonnet
automobile fender	wing
color	colour
realize	realise
program	programme

Technical analysis data

Due to e-learning's dependence on technical infrastructure, courses may have additional technical requirements. Examples of these are assignments to be completed in a required format (e.g., papers and reports to be in a Microsoft Word document or Microsoft Excel workbook) and in a specific versions (e.g., Microsoft Word 2000 and above), cross browser support (e.g., Internet Explorer, Netscape, Mozilla, Safari), or specific Internet browsers for course functionality (Firefox 1.5 and above). Additionally, if access to the Internet is required, is the speed of the access relevant (e.g., dial-up vs. low-speed broadband vs. high-speed broadband) to the student's experience of the course? If the course will be using streaming video, a dial-up connection may be frustrating. On the other hand, if the course is conducted primarily through asynchronous methods such as e-mail and discussion forums, a dial-up connection may be sufficient.

Data collection methods for planning

In addition to determining the type of data that must be collected to insure the course design and development meets the needs of the product and the participants, the method of collecting the data must be determined. End-of-course evaluations from prerequisite courses may gather sufficient data to support the course design and development. In other instances, a survey of potential participants may be required. These surveys may be document forms to be completed by the recipient and returned via e-mail, or in person, or an Internet-based instrument that administers the survey and performs analysis of the results.

Another method of gathering requisite data is through focus groups composed of key course stakeholders. These stakeholders may be potential course participants, potential employers of graduates of the course, key academic personnel, or alumni. A data collection form is recommended to gather consistent data from all focus group participants – whether the participants are in one location and in one group or are from multiple locations and different dates and times.

The data gathered using these collection techniques, along with the analysis of the collected data, provide the foundational facts for the development of the business case, as well as for the course design and development stages of the project.

During the initiating phase, the project team, or at least the sponsor and the project manager, created the business case for the project and identified the scope of the project. The business case will summarize, in a brief document, answers to the who, what, why, and when of the project:

- Who is the project sponsor and project manager?

- What is the project?
- Why is the project being developed and delivered?
- When will the project be completed?

This information will also become an integral part of your project plan.

Determining project team configuration

Whenever possible, the project team members should be identified before creating the project plan. The project manager should first identify the key staff skills that are needed on the project, then determine which resources best provide those skills. Sometimes the desired resources may not be available. In this case, the project manager must take care to insure that the resources, which are available, will meet project requirements. Selecting the team early in the phase will improve the accuracy of estimates and eliminate some risks by building them into the project plan.

The dynamics of selecting project team members has many variables. Questions to consider regarding project team members are:

1 *Must members of the project team be employees?* Many corporations and institutions are moving to an employment model that has a small, permanent body of employees. Services that are not part of daily, on-going operations are contracted on an as-needed basis. An example of this might be a corporate university that has the responsibility to identify development needs, design, and develop courses to fulfill those needs, and to deliver those development opportunities. This institution may have a very small full-time staff with the sole responsibility of managing the corporate university. As needs arise for course design and development, instructional design and development skills are contracted using part-time staff or job-based bids.

2 *Must members of the project team be assigned to the team on a full-time basis?* Are the requirements of some team members such that they are only needed for one phase of the project? A project estimator (a person specializing in estimating the duration of a project), for example, is only required during the planning phase of the project. An instructional designer is only needed during the design stage of course development. In these instances, the estimator or instructional designer would not be full-time team members. They would join the team on an as-needed basis. However, other project team members would be required for the entire duration of the project. The project manager is an example of a full-time team member.

To ensure team success, team guidelines, a meeting schedule, and status reporting standards should be decided upon after the group is first formed. Once the team is assembled, the content and functionality of the project plan can be determined.

Overview of the project management plan

The project management plan describes the necessary steps or actions required to complete the project on time, within budget and to the requirements speci-fied in the project charter. The project management plan is a living document; it is intended to be referenced daily – not placed on the shelf, never to be referenced after it is created.

During the development and execution of the project management plan, unplanned events may occur. For example, a project team member becomes sick, an item purchased from an outside source is delivered late or not as described, time on a system is not available at the previously agreed time, the amount of time on a system is not available in the previously agreed amount, etc. Each of these unplanned events requires a change to the project manage-ment plan. As these changes are managed, the project management plan must be updated to properly reflect the current state of the project.

The scale of the project plan is determined by the project manager by considering the requirements of the project, the project sponsor's input, and/or the requirements identified in the project charter. Additional con-siderations for the contents of the project plan are the nature of the project: is it a short two-week effort or a longer multi-year project. Considering these variables, the sections of the project plan will vary at the discretion of the project manager.

The project management plan sections are:

1   *Scope definition* – based on the preliminary project scope statement, the scope definition is a full description of the project. It must remain true to the preliminary project scope statement but will be enhanced with informa-tion and requirements identified during requirement identification in the analysis stage of ADDIE. Additional enhancements to the preliminary project scope statement may be identified by discussions with the sponsor

Scope Definition
Work Breakdown Structure
Risk Management Plan
Change Management Plan
Schedule
Budget
Staffing Plan
Communication Management Plan
Procurement Plan

Figure 3.2 The project management plan sections.

and stakeholders as well as investigation of the assumptions and constraints identified in the project charter.

2   *Work breakdown structure* – the work breakdown structure (WBS) is a deliverable-based decomposition of the project. It describes each deliverable (report, prototype, system, etc.) that is created or updated as a result of the project. The process of developing the WBS is the foundation for creating cost estimates, budget, time estimates, project schedule, and resources (human and physical) required to complete the project. The WBS will be covered in more detail later in this chapter.

3   *Risk management plan* – the risk management plan is the result of the project team identifying potential risks, analyzing those risks quantitatively and qualitatively, and planning responses to those potential risks. Risk management planning will be covered in more detail later in this chapter.

4   *Change management plan* – changes to the project scope, sometimes called scope creep, are the most common cause for troubled projects. The change management plan defines the process used to submit a request for a change to the project, the form to use to request that change, and the process the project team will use to evaluate and respond to the request for change. Change management planning will be covered in more detail later in this chapter.

5   *Schedule* – the project schedule, at the most general level, lists the planned date of the project start and project finish. It typically lists the start and finish dates of the each of the deliverables of the WBS. Project scheduling and the use of project scheduling tools will be covered in more detail later in this chapter.

6   *Budget* – the budget for the project, at the most general level, lists costs of the project. Similar to the project schedule, it may list the cost of each deliverable of the WBS and should include the cost of new equipment purchased to complete the project, the prorated cost of personnel allocated to the project, and the cost of internal equipment used to develop the project (e.g., computer systems – both desktop and servers).

7   *Staffing plan* – the staffing plan identifies the number and skills of people needed to complete the project. Ideally, it describes these people by skill (e.g., instructional design, developer, graphic design, and system design) vs. a particular person by name. Additionally, the staffing plan identifies the dates the resource is needed and the amount of that resource required (e.g., instructional design – 12 June through 26 June 6.5 hours per day).

8   *Communication management plan* – the communication management plan defines the type of and need for information by the stakeholders, when they need that information, and how the information will be given to them. Examples of the types of communication are:

•   project status report;

- project performance report – work performance, forecasted completions, approved requests for change, and completed deliverables.

9   *Procurement plan* – the procurement plan defines the resources planned to be purchased, the planned purchase date, and the process used to request and evaluate potential suppliers.

Scope definition

When you define the scope of a project, you set the "boundaries" – what is included and what is excluded. To help you scope the project, ask yourself some questions.

- What is the project responsible for delivering? What is the project *not* going to deliver?
- What are the main objectives? Why are you doing it?
- What needs to change in order to achieve these objectives?
- What will the effect of those changes be?
- What will stay the same?
- Which stakeholders will be affected and how?
- What other work or projects are there which might impact on this? (You must agree on boundaries, avoid duplication or omission of tasks or deliverables.)
- Whose responsibility is it to put in place longer term mechanisms/reviews to evaluate the project?

The answers to these questions will help you define the scope of the project and the interfaces you will need to establish with other projects and stakeholders. Knowing what is included and what is excluded is fundamental for planning a project.

Why scope definition is important

Two of our top 20 reasons for project failure are based on scope:

1   Failure to create an organizational context with clearly delineated roles and responsibilities for the e-learning development team and the other stakeholders in the e-learning project.
2   Failure to set forth an e-learning strategy, in the project scope, that takes into account the most pressing business needs of your organization.

Even if you know that the scope is likely to change, it is still important to set out your current understanding of the objectives, what is included and (even more importantly) excluded. This will help you to plan and estimate the resources you require to do the job. Defining and getting broad agreement to the scope definition will help you to:

- ensure clear project goals and objectives;
- promote understanding among all stakeholders;
- reduce ambiguities and risks;
- identify the outcomes you really want;
- manage expectations;
- get management and colleagues' commitment; and
- develop quality and evaluation criteria.

The work breakdown structure (WBS)

When the scope definition has been completed, a high-level plan of milestones can be developed. By expanding on what it will take to achieve the milestones (deliverables, activities, and tasks), the team should construct a work breakdown structure (WBS). The WBS can then be enhanced by sequencing the activities, adding durations and resources after the necessary activities have been agreed upon.

The WBS of the project divides the output of the project into a comprehensive set of deliverables. Any deliverable not described in the work breakdown structure is outside the scope of the project. Examples of these deliverables may be:

- needs analysis report
- instructional design report
- deployment plan
- development status report
- course prototype
- pilot offering attendance report
- formative evaluation report
- e-learning course
- summative evaluation report.

Figure 3.3 highlights the ADDIE process stages and how the data derived from those processes may inform the corresponding WBS deliverables.

The objective of the WBS is to identify required deliverables from the project, and to break these deliverables into subcomponents. This breakdown to the subcomponent level will then help to increase the accuracy of time and cost estimates for the subcomponents. These deliverables may be sequenced in a similar way to the course development process, as illustrated in Figure 3.3, or they may be sequenced in some other manner that best meets the need of your organization. Once the initial legs of the WBS have been identified, potential subcomponents of the deliverables should be brainstormed, as in Figure 3.4.

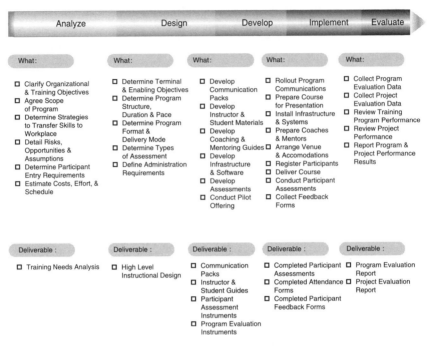

Figure 3.3 ADDIE process design and corresponding WBS deliverables.

Based on the knowledge and experience of the project manager and the subject matter experts, continue identifying subcomponents (see Figure 3.4) until the duration of time required to complete the subcomponent is reasonable. In most e-learning projects, a duration of multiple months is probably too long, whereas a duration of two weeks is more appropriate. The objective of decomposing the deliverables into subcomponents is to enable the project team to make accurate cost and duration estimates for project deliverables and the activities that develop project deliverables. Once the deliverable has been decomposed into its requisite activities, a sequence of execution may be determined.

Resource estimating

Resource estimating is the process of determining what resources (people, equipment, and material) is needed, and in what quantities those resources are used, and finally when the resources will be required to complete the activity. Resource estimation tools include:

- expert judgment by groups or individuals with expert knowledge in the subject matter;

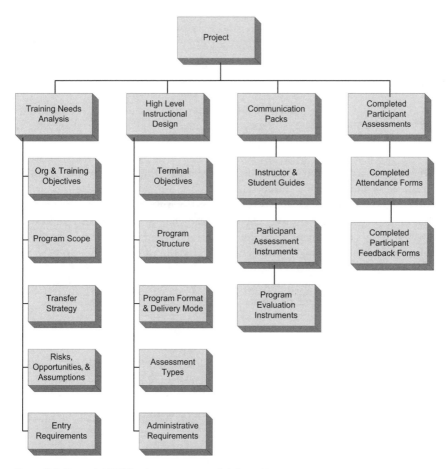

Figure 3.4 Potential WBS subcomponents of deliverables.

- literature review for published best practices;
- bottom-up estimating – a continued decomposition of the activity until a reasonably confident resource estimate is determined; the sum of these resource estimates is used as the resource estimate for the activity.

Once resource estimating is completed, activity duration may be estimated.

Activity duration estimating, the amount of time to complete an activity, may be estimated using the following techniques:

- expert judgment by groups or individuals with expert knowledge in the subject matter;
- analogous estimating by using the actual duration of a similar project

activity that has completed successfully, i.e., using historical information or a project management knowledge base;

- parametric estimating by using a known rate for a unit of measure; an example of parametric estimating is using expert knowledge that it typically takes 10 hours to develop a course module given three module objectives and all the relevant texts;
- three-point estimating based on the development of three activity estimates; a most likely estimate, a pessimistic estimate, and an optimistic estimate.

Of these techniques, analogous and parametric estimating might be applied in the early phases of the project when less information is known about the project. Expert judgment and three-point estimating might be applied in this planning phase of the project when the team has expanded with additional team members or when additional information is available upon which to base the refined estimate. Finally, project teams may choose to add a cushion to the estimate – known as a reserve estimate – to activities with a perceived high risk. Alternatively, the team may choose to create a reserve activity or subcomponent for the purpose of adding a cushion to the time estimate.

Activity decomposition

Decomposition involves subdividing the major project deliverables into smaller, more manageable components until the deliverables are defined in sufficient detail to support project phases.

Decomposition involves the following major steps:

1   Identify the milestones of the project.
2   Decide if adequate cost and duration estimates can be developed at this level of detail for each milestone. If these estimates cannot be determined, the activities should be decomposed into smaller tasks and reviewed for adequate estimates.
3   Identify the elements of the deliverable for all decomposed milestones in tangible, verifiable results in order to facilitate performance measurement.
4   Verify the correctness of the decomposition.

This decomposition, and the subsequent resource scheduling and budgeting, is probably one of the most difficult tasks for the team to undertake. A consideration when determining the sequence of activities is the concept of activity dependency – the relationship of two activities. Determining when a successor activity is able to start relative to the predecessor activity is required as you develop your schedule. It is important to have an accurate reflection of these dependencies in order to provide the smoothest possible execution and control phase of the project. Fortunately, there are several ways you might choose to help you determine how this scheduling would work best.

Time and cost estimating techniques

Estimating work times provides several benefits for the project manager. It gives an idea of the level of effort required to complete a project. This information then enables the project manager to produce a realistic plan based upon that effort. Estimating also helps the project manager anticipate the budget for the project.

There are many formal techniques available to estimate time and cost for activities (see tools section p. 46). Anyone reviewing these estimates should understand that they are approximations, not accuracies.

Although the formal techniques are very specific, most of them have the following tasks in common:

- Break activities down into small pieces for easier and more accurate estimation (part of the WBS).
- Review historical information and compare to current activities.
- Include a contingency buffer for potential risks.
- Solicit advice from others that have previously completed similar activities.
- Identify and document the assumptions and parameters used to derive the estimates.

Expert judgment

Expert judgment will often be required throughout this phase. Such expertise may be provided by any group or individual with specialized knowledge or training and is available from many sources including:

- personal experience
- other teams within your organization
- vendors
- universities or corporations with similar projects.

Project templates

An activity list, or a portion of an activity list from a previous project, is often usable as a template for a new project. In addition, the activity list for a WBS element from the current project may be usable as a template for other similar WBS elements. If you belong to a project management organization, you may be able to find directories of project templates similar to yours. Many project management organizations hold large conferences as well as support local chapters and specific interest groups that do share project templates.

Formal tools to help present resources, tasks, dependencies

A number of tools may be used to assist you with brainstorming and tracking resources, tasks, and their dependencies. We will review the most popular ones here.

Gantt charts

Gantt charts (Figure 3.5) provide a standard format for displaying project schedule information by listing project activities and their corresponding start and finish dates in a **calendar** format. Typical symbols used in the charts include:

- **thick black bars**: summary tasks;
- **lighter horizontal bars**: durations of tasks;
- **arrows**: dependencies between tasks.

Milestones chart

A milestone is a significant event – especially the presentation of a deliverable. Milestones are useful tools for setting schedule goals and monitoring progress. They are critical in large projects. Examples include the completion and customer sign-off on key documents, and the completion of specific products. A milestone chart appears similar to a Gantt chart in its presentation, but it adds the additional specific information of the WBS tasks as illustrated in Figure 3.6.

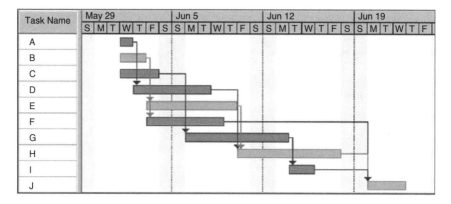

Figure 3.5 Gantt chart example.

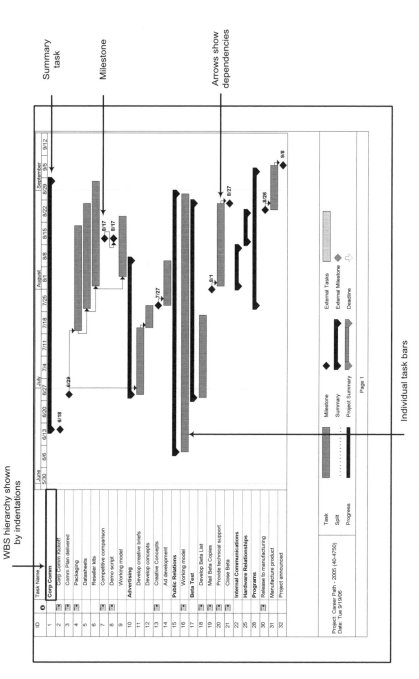

Figure 3.6 Milestones chart example.

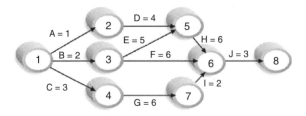

Note: Assume all durations are in days.

Path 1: A-D-H-J   Length = 1 + 4 + 6 + 3 = 14 days
Path 2: B-E-H-J   Length = 2 + 5 + 6 + 3 = 16 days
Path 3: B-F-J   Length = 2 + 4 + 3 = 9 days
Path 4: C-G-I-J   Length = 3 + 6 + 2 + 3 = 14 days

Since the critical path is the longest path through the network diagram, path 2. B-E-H-J, is the critical path for Project X.

Figure 3.7 Critical path diagram example.

Critical path (CPM)

CPM is a network diagramming technique used to predict total project duration (Figure 3.7). A critical path analysis looks at the series of activities that determines the various times in which the project can be completed based on dependencies. The critical path then is the *longest path* through the network diagram and has the least amount of slack or float.

When all activity information has been collected, allocated resources should be assigned to each activity. This will create an initial project schedule. At this point, the schedule may need to be revised to reflect the impact of allocated resources. Estimated one-time and recurring expenditures should also be documented when appropriate.

Throughout the activity and resource definition activities, risks should be looked at as possible additional constraints to the project. The risks should be identified so that appropriate responses can be developed and integrated into the schedule.

Project management software

Project schedules may be created by hand or using project management software. Smaller projects may not need complex diagrams, resource and activity schedules, Gantt charts and milestones charts. A simple spreadsheet may suffice. However, once the e-learning project gets beyond a few single courses – as often happens in projects where entire degree or certificate programs are being developed and delivered – then some type of project management software may be very useful.

Project management software assists project managers by providing a means for organizing project information. A project manager uses the software to enter and maintain a work plan that organizes activities and details. The software calculates the scheduled dates for tasks based on the time or work requirements of each task using a calendar of working days for the project and its resources.

Many programs assist project managers in creating a WBS, PERT (program evaluation review technique) charts, Gantt charts, and resource histograms. Other reports and charts are also readily available for use and customization.

Though using this software can be helpful, it must be stressed that project management software, either desktop- or server-based, does not develop a project management plan. Project management software may be used to develop a project schedule and potentially will create a list of required resources and a budget, if costs have been entered for resources. The principles outlined above are requisite to the correct use of project management software. There are many options for desktop project management software, a few of the most popular ones are:

- Microsoft Office Excel – used to record and compute activity resource requirements and activity duration estimates; Excel may be used manually to create graphic timelines of the project schedule as well.
- Mindjet MindManager – used to brainstorm and capture ideas and create project schedules and track progress.
- Microsoft Office Project – used to create a WBS, sequence activities, record activity resource estimates, record activity duration estimates, and to create project schedules.
- Primavera SureTrak Project Manager – used to create project schedules and manage resources for small to medium projects.
- Deltek Open Plan – used to create project schedules and manage resources.

In addition, there are also enterprise-based project management software programs that cost thousands of dollars. These are usually purchased by large organizations who have project management offices and permanent staff who manage multiple organizational projects.

Risk management planning

The risk management plan is the result of the project team identifying potential risks, analyzing those risks quantitatively and qualitatively, and planning responses to those potential risks. Examples of potential risks mentioned previously are: a project team member becomes sick; an item purchased from an outside source is delivered late or not as described; time on a system is not available at the previously agreed time; and the amount of time on a system is not available in the previously agreed amount.

A four step process is typically used to identify, plan and manage risks.

1   **Identify potential risks**
     During the risk identification process, potential risks are identified by the project team, the project sponsor, stakeholders, subject matter experts, and end users. Techniques used to identify potential risks are:

     • reviews of documentation for this project and previous project;
     • standard group techniques like brainstorming and root cause analysis;
     • interviewing stakeholders; and
     • strength – weakness – opportunity – threat (SWOT) analysis.

2   **Assess potential risks**
     Once risks have been identified, they should be evaluated to determine the probability of occurrence and the impact to the project if the risk does occur. A numerical value may be assigned for the probability of occurrence for each risk. Qualitative risk analysis is used by the team to determine the probability of each risk occurring. Additionally, a numerical value may be assigned to each risk to indicate the impact on the project. Assigning this numerical value is known as "quantitative risk analysis."

3   **Select risk response technique**
     After risk assessment has been performed, response planning for that potential risk should be planned. The following techniques may be used to respond to the risk:

     • Transfer – this technique transfers the risk from the project to another party. Insurance is a form of risk transfer.
     • Avoidance – to use this technique, the activity that might cause the risk is not performed.
     • Mitigation – this technique reduces the severity of the impact. An example of this technique is to develop the course in increments with usability studies at the end of each development cycle. Negative user evaluations on small increments may be handled more easily than at the completion of the final project.
     • Acceptance – this technique is to accept the risk if it occurs. Hopefully, the impact to the project is minimal in this case.

4   **Document in risk management plan**
     Once risks have been identified, assessed, and responses planned, a risk management plan may be created to document the results. Figure 3.8 is an example of a worksheet that may be used to document the risk management plan.

Planning for and managing project risks are extremely important – many organizations have developed or retained subject matter experts on this issue. Additionally, consultancies focused on risk management planning have developed as the importance of project planning has increased.

Risk Management Plan

	Probability	Impact	Proposed Response

Figure 3.8 Worksheet to document the risk management plan.

The change management plan – scope management

Changes to the project scope, sometimes called scope creep, are the most common cause for troubled projects. Scope creep may occur when any change outside of the project charter is recommended. Below are typical changes requested in e-learning systems.

- Users recommend changes after viewing a mock-up of a course page.
- Change needed when the exchange with the school's registration system causes an error.

- The objectives of the course are changed requiring changes throughout the course content, activities, and assessments.
- Functionality that worked in a previous system is not evident in a new system, but is a requirement. Testing tools often fall in this category. For example, the previous system allowed for weighting of multiple-choice responses and the new system does not.

If you recall, the triple constraint triangle introduced in Chapter 2 indicated that an increase in the scope of the project will require an increase to the time and/or cost sides and possibly a decrease in project quality. The **change management plan**, sometimes called the **scope management plan**, section of the project plan describes the process the project team will follow as they receive requests for change. Changes are managed typically through a change request form and a change control process. The change request form might identify the following information:

- date of the request
- name of the person requesting the change
- description of the requested change
- reason for the requested change
- effect of the change on project cost
- effect of the change on project schedule.

A change control process will document the procedures to submit the change request form and the process the project team will use to evaluate each request for change. A sample form is illustrated in Figure 3.9 and available as a template on the website (http://routledge.com/textbooks/9780415772204). Additionally, the process will outline the need for a change control record to document each request for change, along with the status (open, closed, rejected, accepted) of each requested change.

Change management is an important and complex process with any project. All projects experience change from the moment of inception through the close of the project. Most project managers report that the most difficult aspect of change management is working with and managing the stakeholders as each change occurs. Because of the importance of this part of project management, we have devoted an entire chapter later in this book to more fully discuss this people management part of the process (see Chapter 8).

Budget

The project charter committed a not-to-exceed budget value – now is the time to develop the complete budget. The WBS is a great spot to start on this effort. The WBS identifies all deliverables for the course, including the tasks and activities that complete that deliverable. To prepare the budget, identify costs for

Project Change Request Form

DESCRIPTION OF REQUEST WITH REASONS

CHANGES REQUIRED IN KEY PROJECT AREAS

Category	Variance from plan	Proposed change
Scope		
Time		
Cost		
Quality		
Risk		
Communications		

Figure 3.9 Change request form example.

Continued overleaf

BUDGET IMPLICATIONS

```
┌─────────────────────────────────────────────────────┐
│                                                     │
│                                                     │
│                                                     │
│                                                     │
│                                                     │
│                                                     │
└─────────────────────────────────────────────────────┘
```

STEERING BOARD RECOMMENDATION

```
┌─────────────────────────────────────────────────────┐
│ Change accepted, add to plan                        │
│                                                     │
│ Approved by:                                        │
│                                                     │
│ Date:                                               │
│                                                     │
│ Management assigned to:                             │
│                                                     │
└─────────────────────────────────────────────────────┘
```

```
┌─────────────────────────────────────────────────────┐
│ Change deferred / rejected                          │
│ State reasons with examples                         │
│                                                     │
│                                                     │
│                                                     │
└─────────────────────────────────────────────────────┘
```

Figure 3.9 continued

each resource used to complete that deliverable. Costs for all resources must be included. The list of resources and their corresponding cost are illustrated in Table 3.4.

To create the budget, identified costs for each project phase and ADDIE stage could be entered into a spreadsheet program. When all budgetary items have been entered into the spreadsheet, costs for each of the project phases and ADDIE stages may easily be computed. Additionally, charges may be tracked during the project executing phase to ensure that cost overruns do not occur. Many desktop project management software programs allow for the identification of resources and the unit cost of that resource. When the resource is allocated to an activity, hopefully identified in the WBS, the corresponding cost for that resource is also allocated to the activity. Using this functionality of the desktop project management application will create a comprehensive budget.

Table 3.4 Resources and corresponding costs

Resource	Corresponding Costs
• Internal personnel	Fully burdened hourly cost – wages plus overheads (benefits, other allocated charges)
• Contracted personnel	Contracted cost of personnel
• Software	Cost of purchased software or allocated cost of existing software
• Hardware	Cost of purchased hardware or allocated cost of existing hardware
• Facilities (space)	Cost of leased project team space or allocated space
• Infrastructure	Cost of leased infrastructure or allocated infrastructure
• Material	Cost of planned material purchases (e.g., binders, paper, etc.)

Staffing plan

Similar to the development of the budget, a staffing plan should be developed. This staffing plan should identify the type of resource required, the time period for which the resource is required, and the number of hours the resource is required. Typically, the identification of personnel is by skill (e.g., instructional designer, instructional developer, programmer, etc.) and not by an actual person's name. These resources were identified in the budget created above, so the action needed here is to merely document the requirement for each skill. The requirement might be documented in a word-processed document, a spreadsheet, or in a project management application.

When all skill sets have been entered into the document or spreadsheet, hourly time commitments for each of the project phases and ADDIE stages may be easily computed. Additionally, these work hours may be tracked during the project executing phase to ensure that time overruns do not occur. Many desktop project management software programs allow for the identification of skill sets (actually resources to the desktop application) and the unit cost of that skill set. When the skill set is allocated to an activity, hopefully identified in the WBS, the corresponding number of hours for that skill set is also allocated to the activity. Using this functionality of the desktop project management application will create a staffing plan. This plan will show the number of hours needed for each project phase and ADDIE stage allocated to each WBS activity – this may be reported as a resource histogram.

Communication management plan

The purpose of the communication management plan is to identify and plan communication to key stakeholders to address their issues and use their preferred method of communication. To create the communication plan, the project team should identify key stakeholders and brainstorm the stakeholder's potential issues regarding the e-learning course. Upon identifying an issue, the team should capture the key message to convey that will address the issue and the preferred communication method (document, conversation, or meeting). This may be captured in a communication management plan as illustrated in Figure 3.10.

Evaluation plan – picking the right things to measure

Evaluation during product development, as well as upon release of the course, is crucial to the success of the project. Two types of evaluation are common in most projects: formative and summative. Evaluation of the course during its development is formative evaluation.

Formative evaluation

Formative evaluation (also known as internal evaluation) is a method of judging the worth of a program while the program activities are *forming* (in progress). This part of the evaluation focuses on the process. Thus, formative evaluations are often done on the fly. They permit the learner and the instructor to monitor how well the instructional objectives are being met. In the case of e-learning development, formative evaluations permit designers and developers to catch deficiencies so that the proper intervention can take place.

In the figure at the beginning of the chapter showing the relationship between ADDIE processes and IPECC deliverables, formative evaluation occurs during the development stage. This formative evaluation may be in the form of an assessment at the end of each course module to insure that the module objectives have been satisfied, and may include an evaluation of the course esthetics and navigation.

Additionally, usability studies may be performed on a prototype created to evaluate course navigation, course esthetics, and/or course graphics. If the usability study is performed by observing individuals from the target audience as they interface with the course, an observation form should be created to ensure that each observer records the individual reliably as well as to ensure that observations of multiple individuals are performed consistently.

Communication Management Plan

Stakeholder	Stakeholder Issue	Key Message	Communication Method
Stakeholder 1	I. Issue 1		
	2. Issue 2		
	3. Issue 3		
Stakeholder 2	I. Issue 1		
	2. Issue 2		
	3. Issue 3		
Stakeholder 3	I. Issue 1		
	2. Issue 2		
	3. Issue 3		
Stakeholder 4	I. Issue 1		
	2. Issue 2		
	3. Issue 3		
Stakeholder 5	I. Issue 1		
	2. Issue 2		
	3. Issue 3		

Figure 3.10 Communication management plan template.

Summative evaluation

The summative evaluation (also know as external evaluation) is a method of judging the worth of a program at the end of the program activities. The focus is on the outcome.

If we refer to Kirkpatrick's (1998) four levels of evaluation, levels one and two (reactive and learning) are formative evaluations while levels three and four (performance and impact) are summative evaluations, as illustrated in Figure 3.11.

The reactive evaluation is a tool to help determine if the objectives can be reached, the learning evaluation is a tool to help reach the objectives, the performance evaluation is a tool to see if the objectives have actually been met, and the impact evaluation is a tool to judge the value or worth of the objectives. Thus, there are four major break points.

Various instruments may be used to collect the data. Typical choices are questionnaires, surveys, interviews, observations, and testing. The model or methodology used to gather the data should be a specified step-by-step procedure. It should be carefully designed and executed to ensure the data is accurate and valid.

Questionnaires are the least expensive procedure for external evaluations and can be used to collect large samples. They should be trialed before using to ensure the recipients of the questionnaire understand their operation the way the designer intended. When designing questionnaires, keep in mind the most important feature is the guidance given for its completion. All instructions should be clearly stated: let nothing be taken for granted.

If your institution does not have a standard reaction evaluation form, we have included one on the website (http://www.routledge.com/textbooks/9780415772204) and illustrated it here (see Figure 3.12). You may use it in its entirety with the appropriate citation, or modify it as needed for your organization's end of course evaluation.

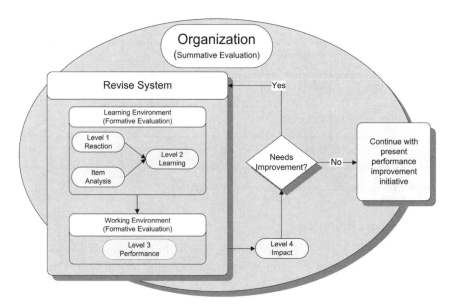

Figure 3.11 Kirkpatrick's four levels of evaluation.

E-learning End-of-Course Evaluation

The University wishes to continue effective, high-quality curriculum. Your input into your experience of this course is very important. All evaluations are submitted anonymously. The instructor will not receive the evaluations until after completion of the term and all grades are mailed. The evaluation results will be compiled, maintaining your anonymity, then presented to the instructor and course developers for improving the course.

Please respond by clicking the number that best matches your opinion on a scale of 0 to 5, where 0 indicates you strongly disagree with the statement, and 5 means you strongly agree with the statement. There is also space for comments at the end of the form.

1. I was able to navigate the course Web pages with ease.	0 1 2 3 4 5
2. My first impression of the course was positive.	0 1 2 3 4 5
3. The identity of the University and the instructor(s) was readily evident.	0 1 2 3 4 5
4. The Web links were relevant and interesting.	0 1 2 3 4 5
5. I was able to view each part of the course in any order.	0 1 2 3 4 5
6. I was required to use several resources (e.g., Web links, textbook(s), chat, bulletin board) to construct knowledge.	0 1 2 3 4 5
7. I was able to interact with my instructor effectively.	0 1 2 3 4 5
8. I was able to interact with my classmates effectively.	0 1 2 3 4 5
9. I was able to post results of my work in a shared space (e.g., bulletin board, Web pages).	0 1 2 3 4 5
10. I was encouraged to use my own initiative to find relevant and timely information pertinent to my studies.	0 1 2 3 4 5

Figure 3.12 Sample end-of-course evaluation.

Summative evaluations may include the course participants, the course product(s), the instructor, and any other aspects of the project after the course or project has come to a close.

Summative evaluation of the released course, clearly identified in Figure 3.12, may follow Kirkpatrick's model of evaluation or may simply be end-of-course evaluations. Many institutions have developed standard course evaluation forms to be used for summative evaluation. You may consider adding additional questions to these instruments in order to evaluate course navigation and usability. If your institution does not have a standard impact evaluation form, you may wish to also consider the free tools from the American Society for Training and Development's (ASTD) 2003 Measurement

Kit: Tools for Benchmarking and Continuous Improvement (http://www.astd.org/NR/rdonlyres/CE8B053B–6651–4339–9A50-CEEE61E75816/0/2004_MeasurementKit_Pt_II.pdf).

As you can see from these samples, one form is used by the participant to evaluate his or her experience of the course. The other sample is used by the participant's supervisor to obtain an alternative perspective.

In addition to measuring customer satisfaction using an end-of-course evaluation, consideration for long-term and/or short-term evaluations must be made.

Critical success factors (CSFs), those items that are crucial to the success of the course, should be identified during the initiation stage of the project management process, considered in the planning stage to ensure that these CSFs are of the utmost importance as the project management plan is developed, and as evaluation plans are developed and executed, these CSFs must be measures. Examples of CSFs might be ease of navigation, availability of the course in multiple languages, cross browser support, the ability to take the course over high- and low-speed Internet connections. Many of these CSFs may have been identified during audience and technical analysis performed during the initiating stage of the project management process. A final evaluation consideration is the evaluation of business productivity.

Evaluation of business productivity is paramount. Examples of business metrics are the number of course participants per month/quarter/year, the profit created due to the delivery of the course, increased skill as measured by increased employee productivity, increased customer satisfaction, and a decrease in the amount of time it takes to install a software application. Ideally, during this stage, plans to measure the business productivity metrics relevant to your institution have been planned.

Project planning summary

The planning phase of the project has one output, the project management plan, which is the input to the executing phase of the project. The contents of the project management plan is a set of plans that, when executed, will ensure completion of the course design and development and delivery within time and budget constraints. At the discretion of the project manager, the project management plan will contain the following items:

1   a scope definition
2   a work breakdown structure
3   a risk management plan
4   a change management plan
5   a project schedule – a project timeline with project milestones
6   a budget for the project

7   a staffing plan
8   a communication management plan
9   a procurement plan.

During the executing phase of the project, Chapter 4 of this text, this project management plan and its sub-plans will be executed to design, develop, and deliver the e-learning project.

Executing the project

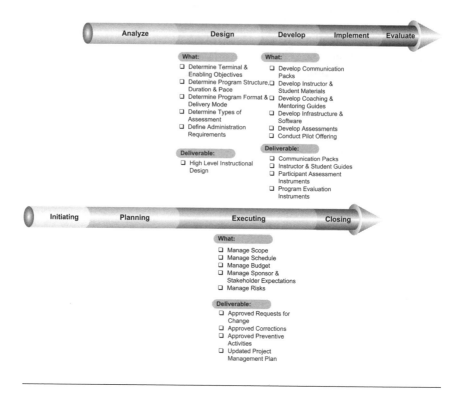

Now that the most difficult work has been done in the initiating and planning phases of your project, it is time to begin executing your plan. In the initial stages, there may have been large spaces of time where seemingly nothing happened, such as waiting for a stakeholder meeting, arranging sponsorship, and getting approval of the plan. However, at this stage, the plan is executed and everything may seem to go very quickly and be in a constant state of flux. This is the point at which the role of the project manager becomes paramount as he or she works through the day-to-day implementation and coordinates the work of the project team.

The executing phase involves implementing the planned activities according to the approved project plan, which also contains the project schedule and budget. This is where the work of the project is actually performed and consumes both resources and time. In this phase, the project manager coordinates the work of the project team. Although this phase basically consists of executing the plan, recording progress, and updating the plan, there are other activities key to project success. These include leading the project team and managing relationships with stakeholders.

In preparing the project team, the project manager needs to make sure that each project team member thoroughly understands the goals and the overall schedule of the project. Equally important is that each member understands their unique relationship to each goal and to the schedule. Leading a successful project team requires the effective use of the resources involved within the project and the development of individual and group skills to enhance project performance. If project team members lack the necessary skills, such skills must be developed when necessary so that each team member can perform their assigned activities.

The project manager is responsible for managing relationships and addressing various types of problems that affect project success. Constant monitoring and control of all aspects of the project will help identify problems. Schedule conflicts (including those resulting from tasks of other high-priority projects), unexpected resource constraints and budget overruns are examples of the types of problems that are common in a project, and that should have been identified in the risk management plan. The project manager must establish a climate of open communication with his/her team members and remove obstacles so that the project will remain on track.

Stakeholders' expectations also need to be managed during this phase. It is important that stakeholders understand and support the project goal and overall schedule. The best way to do this is through open communication, as outlined in the communication management plan, with the stakeholders to assure that they're apprised of project status. It is important to understand stakeholders' viewpoints while addressing their questions and concerns. It may be necessary to persuade or influence a stakeholder to create a higher level of stakeholder confidence in the project.

All of the above are important aspects of the executing phase in any project. In this chapter we are going to look at specific areas of concern in executing an e-learning project. Many of these should be addressed during the planning stage, but may need to be altered during this phase or initially addressed if they weren't part of planning. These alterations should be performed in accordance with the change management plan subsection of the project plan.

ADDIE role in the execution phase of project management

The ADDIE *implementation* stage is the one that most closely integrates with the execution phase of project management. During this phase, your organization is working to deliver your courses to the students. Each course now represents a significant investment of institutional resources and time. Not only must the course look good and operate well, but even more important it must make a significant and meaningful impact on learners.

On the strategic level, organizations rely on training programs to reduce costs and improve profitability by improving both the learner's and the design team's performance in many different ways. Among the expectations for companies interested in profitability are:

- improved efficiency and productivity of employees;
- ensured legal compliance and reduced liability where the company may be at risk in processes or procedures;
- employees are guided through new and changed processes; and
- employees are introduced to the company's methods and culture.

Academic institutions have expectations as well. These include:

- improved efficiency and productivity in course development;
- the ability to provide quality distance-learning to students who cannot come to campus – a quality that is at least equivalent to that achieved in the classroom;
- return on investment in their e-learning infrastructure and development shown by increased enrollment and persistence in degree programs; and
- decreased costs per student – either because of not having to build more structures or because of using faculty time to increase ratios of student to faculty contact.

Organizations that want to achieve any of the above goals need well-written training programs that are launched successfully. However, it's important to remember that great course content doesn't guarantee a successful launch. During the ADDIE implementation stage, the number one difficulty is scope.

How scope impacts training delivery

When institutions deliver training programs, they often involve thousands of learners. Even a single small course can involve dozens of people. Some of the biggest challenges during the ADDIE implementation stage fall into the categories of training administration and logistics.

Some companies have very skilled in-house training departments. These people know how to coordinate and deliver training programs to thousands of people across the world within a short timeframe. However, other institutions – particularly academic institutions – may not have this depth of training delivery experience and a regional, statewide, or nationwide distance course rollout can become quite a challenge.

If you've followed the ADDIE model, you've conducted a course pilot session. Perhaps some learners gathered together in a classroom or tested out the online learning course. You've asked a sample group of learners to help you review the course. However, there's a lot of work to ramp up from this single session to a full-distance course delivery.

In many ways, the course delivery phase must recognize the powerful impact of Murphy's Law – if anything can go wrong, it will. This is why your project management plan must include the training delivery process, and have an excellent change management plan for dealing with all the times Murphy's Law visits your project. Let's look at some of the factors that you should consider when preparing to launch e-learning courses.

An e-learning course often requires significant systems integration tasks. Table 4.1 presents some key questions that must be addressed during this phase of the project.

There are many ways that an e-learning course can create havoc in your infrastructure if you are not prepared. An online course can be so popular that the enrollment crashes your server or the hosting site when everyone tries to access it at the same time. A course at a major university had no cap on enrollment, as the course on campus had never had more than 50 students. When it was made available online, the course enrolled over 700 students and brought the server with the LMS down.

Courses tend to have many links to outside resources and these links are frequently changed. Your help desk is then inundated with calls from students indicating they have a "file not found" error. This may seem like a simple fix, but the stress on your help system, developers, and maintenance personnel until the error is fixed can take up needed time and resources at a critical time in the execution of the project.

These types of issues and many more can be alleviated with a good project plan that includes planning for the execution and, equally important, planning for change and how you will accommodate change during the execution phase. Collaboration between departments and among team members is just as critical during this phase as in any of the preceding phases. The relationships should be strong and working at this point of your project so that you can easily address issues that come up. Let's look at some of the most important considerations during this phase of the project.

Configuration management

At this stage you will have identified at least the specifications for your system, including:

- How you will store and reuse content or learning objects – through a learning content management system (LCMS)?
- Which standards you wish to use to store data, and what your granularity standards are (e.g., SCORM (sharable content object reference model), Dublin Core, IMS)

Table 4.1 Key questions to address during the executing phase

Task	Key Questions
Infrastructure	• Where will the course be hosted (within the institution or contracted with a hosting vendor)? • How much storage space will be required for the e-learning files? • How many learners will need to access the course in total? • How many learners will access the course at any time? • How much bandwidth will be needed (peak use and monthly)? • Will this course need to integrate with an existing LMS? • How will course enrollment and completion data be tracked? • How will course outcomes, test scores, and other evaluation data be tracked and reported? • Is this course SCORM compliant, or does it meet other metadata compliance needs?
Access	• Will learners be able to access the course through the Web or will they need to connect to an intranet? • How will learners connect (dial-up, VPN, through a corporate firewall)? • Can the course recognize the learner's connection speed and optimize course delivery? • Will learners have all necessary applications automatically loaded onto their computers? • Will learners need to download any applications or plug-ins?
Help Desk	• Who will be responsible for security issues related to the course files? • Who will help learners who have difficulties accessing the online course? • Who will answer technical questions? • Who will answer content questions? • Who will be the liaison between students, teachers, developers, and helpdesk personnel?
Enrollment and Security	• How will students be enrolled for the course or program of study? • Will they enroll themselves or will someone enroll them? • How will their identity be verified? • How will course rosters be tracked?
Logistics	• Who will manage training administration? • Who will manage training logistics? • How will course statistics be tracked? • Who will be responsible for collecting and communicating these statistics?

- What type of system will deliver your e-learning courses, track your students, and manage the learning process – the learning management system (LMS) or managed learning environment (MLE).

Depending on what you already specified in the planning stage, you may have already selected these systems and the executing stage includes the actual installation and implementation of these systems.

For others, however, the first step of executing the plan is to select the vendors or open source systems that will eventually meet these needs. In order to do this effectively, you want to make sure you have developed good rubrics for evaluating each candidate system and a clear process for making the decision and final selection.

How to select a learning content management system (LCMS)

Though your planning process will identify the specific criteria important to your learning environment, there are some helpful rubrics which have already been developed by other organizations facing this task. Additionally, there are organizations whose mission is to evaluate and report on the comparison of systems.

One way to think about evaluating an LCMS is to think of the creation, publishing, and reuse lifecycle that comes into play and evaluating how each of these stages meets your organizational needs. The seven stages of any LCMS lifecycle include:

1 *categorization* – determining an organizational or categorization scheme;
2 *workflow* – assigning a workflow;
3 *creation* – creating content;
4 *repository* – storing content in a repository;
5 *versioning* – tracking multiple versions of the same content;
6 *publishing* – distributing content to a course management system, to web-sites, or directly to users through e-mail or mobile devices;
7 *archiving* – saving content after its usability period for historic purposes.

Figure 4.1 details many of the requirements you may wish to evaluate in selecting the appropriate LCMS and LMS integrated system for your e-learning implementation.

How to choose a learning management system (LMS)

The primary purpose of an LMS is to deliver content to students in a particular format selected by the organization, track the students' progress, and provide

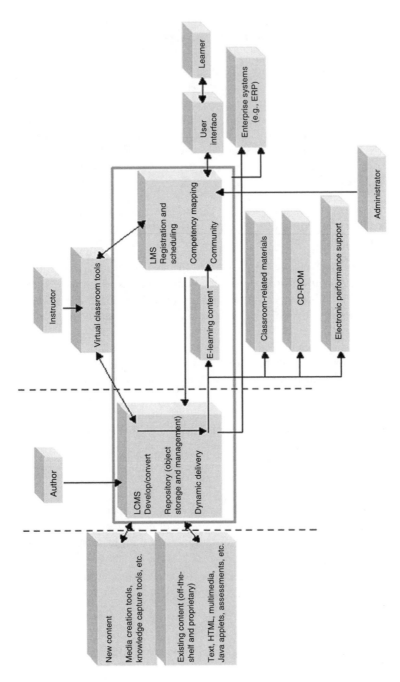

Figure 4.1 LCMS and LMS integration requirements.

opportunities for students and teachers to collaborate as appropriate for the learning environment.

Your planning process should have identified the elements most needed within your institution. Below is a list of common elements many organizations have used for evaluating an LMS.

General criteria

- *Easy access* – how does it work with your other systems? Can students login to only one system or do they need separate passwords and IDs for the LMS?
- *Navigation* – is it easy to locate course content? Is it easy to know how to return to material once it has passed? Can students and teachers easily move from one function to another or put them together in any order they need?
- *Tracking* – does the system allow you to track student progress? Does it allow students to track progress and to always know where they are and what they have already completed?
- *Component integration* – are systems within the LMS integrated so that you don't waste time having to retype information?
- *System architecture* – must be flexible, extensible, and scalable. Flexibility allows your organization to create a unique look and feel for the system (i.e., your logo, your colors). Extensibility allows you to add new functions and features as they become available – for example an integrated portfolio building tool. Scalability allows the system to grow without compromising its performance or having to switch to a new one.
- *Security* – must provide users with unique IDs and passwords and their distribution must be secure. Encryption keys are used to allow for sender and receiver communication but minimizing risk of a third party intercepting sensitive information. In addition there should be security attached to UserIDs that allow access only to qualified levels identified at time of entry.

Student management system

- *Access* – is it easy to create and issue access to the system? Will the system integrate with other current access mechanisms your institution uses (e.g., LDAP, CAS)?
- *Organization* – is it flexible to allow you to organize administrators, teachers, and/or students into groups for reporting, content assignment, or overall course management?
- *Registration* – how does the registration system interact with the access properties, and how does it integrate with whatever registration system your institution already uses?

- *Class/course management* – how does it allow all course-related resources such as classrooms, instructors, and common materials (e.g., tutorials, library access, instructions to all students) to inter-relate?
- *Tracking/reporting* – what levels of student progress and activity are tracked? Can you define incremental development/knowledge goals and report on those separate from entire course completion? Can you track and verify mandated compliance training?

Content management

- *Organizational structure* – does it allow for you to determine an organizational structure that matches your current organization (e.g., by department, by instructor, by coordinator)?
- *Sharing* – is there a way to share content common to more than one course without having to duplicate it, so that a change made to one element is automatically changed in all courses containing that element?
- *Targeting* – can you target content to the correct individuals, groups, or courses?
- *Designators* – can you designate selected content as "required" for a course vs. optional material? Can the same content be designated differently for different courses?
- *Personalization* – can content be organized in any number of paths? Can you personalize the path by course, unit, department, or individual?
- *Assessment* – are there a variety of methods to create, edit, distribute, and deliver assessments? Are these elements easily graded and recorded in a common area that both teachers and individual students may access (i.e., a grade book or progress report)?
- *Tracking* – can you track what content has been accessed, how often, and by whom?

Communication

- *Modes* – are there both synchronous and asynchronous modes of communication available, and are they available in both one-on-one and group formats?
- *Integration* – are communication tools integrated within the LMS, so that each tool reports needed data to the other tools? Are you also able to communicate beyond the LMS (e.g., send e-mail outside the LMS or receive e-mail from outside into the LMS)?
- *Ease of use* – are communication tools easy to access and use, and are they integrated into content options or separate?

Authoring

- *New development* – are you able to develop new courses yourself or do you have to use third-party courses?
- *Templates* – is there a templating capability to speed development? Are you restricted to a few templates provided by the LMS or can you also create and save your own?
- *Standards* – do authored materials conform to industry standards to improve compatibility between course platforms and/or between the LMS and a content repository (e.g., IMS, SCORM, Dublin Core)?

You may wish to look at rubrics others have developed for comparing learning management systems. Two sites that are particularly useful are:

- edutools – a site that reviews products by researching and describing more than 40 product features, available at http://www.edutools.info/course/index.jsp
- **Ocotillo Web Courseware Comparisons and Studies** – a meta site listing many links for courseware comparison sites, available at http://www.mcli.dist.maricopa.edu/ocotillo/courseware/compare.html

The importance of standards compliance

The content of the learning is even more important than the technologies used to deliver the learning. Without content there would be no learning. The type of standard you wish to follow in your project was likely selected in the planning phase. During the execution phase, it is important that the project manager ensures these standards are being followed and used throughout the content development process. For purposes of this book, we are going to use the SCORM standard as our examples. However, the lessons would be the same for whatever standard you might choose for your organizational needs.

The SCORM standard is a relatively easy standard to implement poorly. There are many levels of conformance to consider. Ask yourself these questions:

- Do you know what level you need to achieve organizational and learning objectives?
- Do you know how to structure your learning materials into objects that will provide for the greatest flexibility while minimizing the amount of effort and cost?
- Are you thinking about purchasing a SCORM conversion tool? Do you know if this tool will provide you with the "portability" and "flexibility" you need? Many automated tools do not tag learning objects at the asset or

SCO level. They just "package" and zip files. This may make the learning material SCORM conformant, but you will not be able to reuse or have easy access to learning objects. You must register assets and SCOs to make the objects reusable and accessible.

The Project Manager should work closely with the implementation team to better understand the requirements, including business objectives, budget, learning processes, technical and design requirements. Depending on the size of the project, the team may also need an experienced SCORM project manager, a SCORM data architect, and a senior e-learning designer. This consultative project management process should include:

- *Clarifying business and learning objectives*

    1   What are the key drivers in designing or migrating to the SCORM standard?
    2   What aspects of reusability, accessibility, interoperability, durability are important to you?

- *Meta data requirements*

    1   What data do you want to have tagged?
    2   What level of tagged data is required to achieve objectives?

- *Dynamic (run-time) data requirements*

    1   What dynamic data do you want to gather from the learning process (e.g., bookmarks, time required for assessments)?
    2   What dynamic data do you want to track for reporting purposes?
    3   How do you want to implement/track assessments?
    4   Are these requirements managed by your SCORM compliant LMS or will there be an additional requirement to manage this dynamic data?

- *Design*

    1   At what level of granularity do you want to tag data (e.g., what level is an SCO)?
    2   Based upon your objectives, and your metadata requirements, will changes need to be made to structure or design of the learning materials?

Tools for creating metadata

Metadata is usually created in editors. There are several tools and application interfaces available to assist in tagging your content. Content repositories often come with some type of interface for tagging content. Additionally, there are editors specifically for tagging and packaging content per your specifications. A few of the open source tools available are listed below.

ADLib

http://adlib.athabascau.ca/adlib/ (login required; free registration)

The "ADLib repository provides a metadata entry tool to make the description of learning objects simple enough for the non-specialist. ADLib follows the CanCore Learning Resource Metadata Application Profile(CanCore), a set of guidelines for the uniform description of digital educational resources in Canada."

ALOHA 2

http://aloha2.netera.ca/

"ALOHA II is a Java-based software project that is being undertaken by Netera and the University of Calgary's Learning Commons in partnership with the Bolton Institute in the UK. The project represents part of a suite of tools in the eduSource project. The software has been designed for indexing, aggregating, sharing, multi-purposing, and re-purposing learning objects. It is created to meet the needs of indexers, educators and learners and includes versatile and powerful indexing tools and flexible searching of multiple educational object repositories. The software is based on the educational standards of IMS and SCORM. Currently it is designed to author Learning Object Metadata (LOM), build IMS Content Packages (IMS CP 1.22), build SCORM Sharable Content Objects (SCORM 1.2) and read IMS Vocabulary Definition Exchange (IMS VDEX) files."

Automatic Metadata Generation Framework

http://memling.cs.kuleuven.ac.be/amg/tryIt.php

"The idea behind our framework is that learning object metadata can be derived from two different types of sources. The first source is the learning object itself; the second is the context in which the learning object is used. Metadata derived from the object itself is obtained by content analysis, such as keyword extraction, language classification and so on. The contexts typically are learning (content) management systems (like Blackboard) or author institution information. A learning object context provides us with extra information about the learning object that we can use to define the metadata."

Curriculum Online Tagging Tool (v3x)

http://www.curriculumonline.gov.uk/SupplierCentre/taggingtool.htm

"The Curriculum Online Tagging Tool is designed to make the process of creating metadata and outputting as easy and intuitive as possible for those suppliers who do not already have the means for doing so." A version of this tool is being developed to support UK LOM Core and aspects of CanCore.

"The tagging tool enables you to create and store details about your learning resources. It also allows you to add these details to the Curriculum Online portal so that teachers can find out about your learning resources. Once you've added details about a resource to the portal you can use the tagging tool to update them at any time, or even remove them completely."

eduSource: eRIB Metatagging Tool

http://demo.licef.teluq.uquebec.ca/eRIB/

"This tool is concordant with the CanCore Guidelines and permits the user to create Metadata records for learning objects stored on a personal computer and thus constituting a personal repository (Repository-in-a-Box, RIB). The eRIB provides all the basic tools to add a new node to the eduSource network. It consists of an open source database (eXist) with a built-in LOM (IEEE Learning Object Metadata) data structure and a set of tools to create, manage and find metadata records in the eduSource Network. Some minimal requirements must be met before installing the eRIB. It exists in English and in French."

"To create your personal eRib, please download necessary software from http://edusource.licef.teluq.uquebec.ca/ese/en/install_erib.htm."

EXPLOR@-II LCMS and Learning Object Repository

http://explora2.licef.teluq.uquebec.ca/demo/

"Explor@ ™-II is a software environment for the delivery of courses or distance learning events on the Internet. It allows creating a virtual training centre that delivers a set of courses on the Internet according to a variety of models and using a LO repository facilitating information access, production, follow-up and coaching of learners as well as training management. The LOR is fully compatible with the IEEE LOM, Cancore and Normetic. A demo version is available at http://explora2.licef.teluq.uquebec.ca/demo/ you may use the username and password DEMO to access the site."

LOMPad

http://demo.licef.teluq.uquebec.ca/LomPad/

"Developed by the LICEF / COGIGRAPH Team, the LomPad is available for free as open source code for educational purposes. This tool allows the user to tag objects according to several major application profiles, namely LOM/IEEE, NORMETIC, CanCore and SCORM. The LomPad interface is bilingual, French and English."

Reload v2.0

http://www.reload.ac.uk/index.html

"The tool supports all aspects of the latest and previous versions of IMS Content Packaging, including IMS Meta-data with IEEE LOM (Learning Object Metadata) vocabulary. It enables content to be aggregated into different structures and tagged with meta-data for exchange between systems and delivery to learners. A package viewer is to be incorporated to enable both authors and learners to interact with packages produced. Includes the functionality to edit level A Learning Design manifests as well as Content Packages and Metadata records." Moreover, it includes the following tools:

- SCORM Player
- IMS Learning Design Editor (Levels A, B &C)
- IMS Learning Design Player.

Note: The metadata editor is accessible in all these tools.

Component integration

Component integration is that phase which ensures that all parts of the e-learning product work together. The objective of this phase is to prove that the developed system satisfies the requirements defined in your project plan. Several types of tests will be conducted in this phase. First, subsystem integration tests are executed and evaluated by the development team to prove that the program components integrate properly into the subsystems and that the subsystems integrate properly into an application. Next, the testing team conducts and evaluates system tests to ensure the developed system meets all technical requirements, including performance requirements. Next, the testing team and the security program manager conduct security tests to validate that the access and data security requirements are met. Finally, users participate in acceptance testing to confirm that the developed system meets all user requirements as stated in the project plan. Acceptance testing shall be done in a simulated "real" user environment with the users using simulated or real target platforms and infrastructures.

Typical tasks and activities performed during component testing and integration

The tasks and activities actually performed depend on the project planning document and the complexity of the project. The following basic tasks should be completed during the integration and test phase:

- *Establish the test environment* – Establish the various testing teams and ensure the test systems and requirements are ready. Create test scenarios or use cases that simulate the actual end user developer, teacher, and learner experience.
- *Conduct integration tests* – This may include creating/loading test databases and executing integration tests. The test sets may include full courses or individual learning objects, or some combination of the two. This is to ensure that program components integrate properly into the subsystems and the subsystems integrate properly into a delivered application or learning experience.
- *Conduct security testing* – Execute security (penetration) tests. This is again done through creating and loading test databases and use cases. Security may include anything from basic access, to typical cheating scenarios, to serious fraudulent access and use of student data, curriculum information, assessments, and final grades. Ensure that any data passed from one system to another (i.e., from the LMS to the registrar or transcript system) is also secure.
- *Conduct acceptance testing* – The acceptance testing is usually done in pilot with actual users to ensure all issues are addressed and functioning properly.
- *Create/revise documentation* – During this phase, any operations or systems administration manuals, user manuals, training plans, maintenance manuals, conversion plans, implementation plans, contingency plans, etc. are created and/or updated.
- *Deliverables* – Component integration and testing frequently yields a number of possible deliverables. These include:

  1 Test analysis reports – document each unit/module, subsystem integration, as well as system and user acceptance and security.
  2 Test analysis approval determination – reports on the final result of the test reviews and testing levels in the component integration. It briefly summarizes the perceived readiness for migration of the software from a test environment to a production environment.
  3 Test problem reports – document problems encountered during testing.
  4 Security certifications/accreditations – documents any certifications needed to ensure security before the system becomes production/operational. In large systems this may include: system security plan; rules of behavior; configuration management plan; risk assessment;

security test and evaluation; contingency plan; privacy impact assessments; and the certification and accreditation memorandums.

Upon completion of all integration and testing tasks, and receipt of resources
for the next phase, the project manager, together with the project team, should
prepare and present a project status review for the decision-maker and project
stakeholders. The review should address:

- integration and test activities status;
- planning status for all subsequent life cycle phases (with significant
  detail on the next phase, to include the status of pending contract
  actions);
- resource availability status; and
- acquisition risk assessments of subsequent lifecycle phases given the
  planned acquisition strategy.

Vendor/contractor selection and contracting

Most institutions find they need to contract with vendors and contractors
for one or more phases of the project. This may range from actually contracting out the entire project management for building an e-learning environment to keeping it in-house but looking for an LMS vendor or a CMS
vendor.

There are many reasons you might choose to outsource some or all of your
e-learning project needs. According to an EDUCAUSE Center for Applied
Research (ECAR) survey (2002), higher education institutions indicated operating efficiencies and lack of in-house skills as the primary reasons to outsource.
These are also the main reasons why corporations and government entities
outsource. As illustrated in Figure 4.2, additional reasons were cost savings and
access to innovative services.

Key considerations for selecting vendors and outsourcing

Selecting a vendor or contracting for outsourced services should be carefully
considered in e-learning, as you will likely be stuck with your selection for a
minimum of five years. Most e-learning environments take 12–18 months to
complete the technical implementation. Simultaneously, it takes approximately
two years to make sure faculty, staff, developers, designers, and administrators
are trained and able to use the system. Then you need to actually use the system
in production for a couple of years to work out best practices and see if it meets
your needs. So any commitment you make at this stage may be, in effect, at least
a five-year commitment. It is not to be taken lightly.

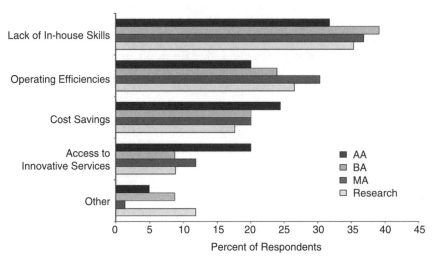

Figure 4.2 Reasons to outsource by institution type.

Contractor selection

When selecting a vendor or contractor to assist with your project, you need to first determine what level of interaction with your team is necessary. You also need to define the contractor's scope of work and how it relates to the rest of the project. Here are some key considerations.

You need more than a multimedia development company

If the contractor is tasked with developing and delivering courses or course content, make sure the vendor is not just a multimedia or Web company, but one who has experience in instructional design. Otherwise you may get a lot of glitz and glam that looks nice but does a poor job of actually teaching the topic or helping students to learn.

Source code and copyright should belong to the project

Make sure the contractor will turn over all source code for maintenance, and that the copyright to the content and code remains with you (or is at least shared).

No rendering or code generation engines should be required

Be clear that you will not accept a product that is based on a vendor-specific "black box" or engine. For example, some contractors have an XML rendering engine that they sell with the finished product. Others have an engine that generates JavaScript that is interpreted by that engine. Without that engine, the product will not display properly. This means that you are forever forced to pay license fees on that engine and if you move to another platform that doesn't use XML, you will have difficulty getting any vendor-created content to run.

Specify all acceptable languages and tools

Specify the programming language or development tools the contractor will use to create your materials (e.g., Java, PhP, C++, Flash, Director, Toolbook, specific testing software). If you are to maintain the developed objects, you need to ensure it will be compatible with your systems and with your programming developers' expertise. If you have agreed to languages or tools not currently known by your project team, then a part of that vendor contract might include that they train your team in the use of those languages and tools for post-development maintenance requirements.

A full-time, knowledgeable contact person is needed

Verify that the vendor has full-time, on-site staff for all critical project tasks. Many vendors use contract labor or part-time labor on jobs. This isn't a problem for discrete content development. However, for your critical tasks and for integration of project elements, you want to be sure you can contact the person responsible during normal business hours.

Prototyping/creating e-learning materials

The crux of the entire e-learning execution phase is the actual creation and delivery of learning objects or course materials. We could write an entire book or two on how to create effective online learning materials. However, that is not the intent of this book or of this chapter. We will review some key concepts of instructional design and then focus on those aspects that are critical to the project management of course content creation, testing, execution, and evaluation.

During the planning phase of project management you will have been asking yourself some key questions about course design, development, and delivery that impact the execution of that design at this point. Those questions should be asked again here as you begin the actual development process.

- Is e-learning appropriate for my audience and topic? Should it be taught 100 percent online or in some alternative blended format?
- How much interactivity is appropriate for my audience, topic, budget? Is there demonstrable return that I can use to justify greater budget?
- How can I provide a development process, tools, and systems that foster

informal learning in a way that I know will have impact on the performance that I care about and that is repeatable?

- What does this look like in practice and when do I use it within a course?
- What effect does the course have on the students, and how do I measure that effect?
- What can I borrow from other related theories of design – knowledge management, collaborative learning, student-centered design – that makes sense for this project?
- What can I borrow for other management practices that will help make this process go smoothly?
- What systems, tools, and techniques can I use to help students become better learners?
- What types of links, references, research, additional materials can I provide both as remediation and advanced resources?
- Can I reduce the duration of courseware and still get an effective result?

E-learning courses differ from traditional classroom courses in several ways. Since students do not have non-verbal cues or the ability to raise a hand to ask immediate questions, the course must contain learning activities with explicit instructions. Above all, the writing *must* be clear. This includes writing instructions, orientations, expectations, as well as the actual topical content.

Online courses are, by nature, learner-centered and can have more active participation by all students in the class than in a traditional classroom. Without the structure of weekly classes, students are expected to take a more active role in their own learning. A fundamental difference between online and traditional classes is that students make their presence known not only by simply showing up, but by actually having to do something – for example, submit an assignment, ask a question, participate in a discussion. Opportunities for these interactions with the course materials, with the instructor, and with other students must be designed into the e-learning classroom.

Keep it simple

The field of instructional design and e-learning contains a plethora of articles about the abundance of time it takes to develop an online course. This can be frighteningly true, and your project can quickly get out of hand if you don't carefully stick to your design plan. Both faculty and design staff are frequent contributors to "scope creep." This is where the scope of the project grows to include additional features or requirements that were not determined in advance. A certain amount of scope creep is inevitable and should be incorporated into your project plan. However, you need to have a clear idea of how much is too much and will take you over time and over budget.

Like any expert in their field, good instructional designers and faculties have a view of the world that provides for the perfect course for every student. Though this is a laudable goal, it is an unrealistic one in the real world. The perfect course for every student would be highly complex, variable, and ultimately very costly. This is why it is very important to have asked and answered the questions posed above. Then, based on your answers, you must determine how much perfection you can afford in time and budget.

Large e-learning instructional design projects can learn something here from the lessons of extreme programming. Extreme programming is a method used by software developers, working in small to medium-sized teams, to develop software in the face of vague or rapidly changing requirements. Instructional design is often done in face of variable techniques, unknown or changing requirements, and is almost always needed yesterday. So, there are some lessons to share.

The first rule of design in extreme programming is to always have the simplest design that meets the needs of the project. Let's look at what is the simplest design that meets the needs of e-learning instruction.

The first step in keeping it simple is to determine the criteria for success for your course project. These criteria are not specific topic objectives or knowledge-base outcomes. Instead they are the minimal expectations of every course or learning object that is developed within your project. The following items represent the type of generic criteria that a well-developed e-learning course might include:

1 clearly articulated objectives and expectations;
2 an easily navigable web site;
3 a course structure that facilitates collaborative learning;
4 assignments and activities that facilitate participation and communication among students, as well as between students and the instructor;
5 timely feedback for students from the instructor;
6 an appropriate use of technologies to enhance learning;
7 a discussion space for learners to talk openly about the course (expectations, uncertainty, what they like, dislike, their participation, progress, etc.);
8 an appropriate form of assessment that provides feedback regarding the student's progress toward outcomes and goals.

To some reading this book, they'll look at this list and think "that doesn't sound very simple." They would be right. Simple design does not necessarily mean simple execution. Good design is never easy, but the expression of the design should be simple.

Extreme programming also offers some principles that help work the simple design strategy. These principles may help e-learning designers as well.

1 *Make small initial investments* – You should make the smallest possible

investment in the design before getting payback for it. For example, if your goal is for a student to memorize all the bones in the hand, then the smallest investment would be to assign a reference paper and test their memorization. That meets the objective. A larger investment might be to provide an interactive image of the hand with all the bones identified and to provide an interactive, electronic flashcard study guide to help them memorize the bones prior to taking the assessment. What is your goal? What is your time and budget? Both provide payback.

2   *Assume simplicity* – You should assume that the simplest design you can imagine possibly working actually will work. In the above example, the assessment of memorization doesn't require the beautiful image. However, if your goal is for them not only to memorize but to recognize where these bones are located and point to them, then the most simple design may be the image with the interactive pieces. By choosing the simplest design, it will give you time to do a thorough job in case the design doesn't work. In the meantime, you won't have to carry along the cost of extra complexity.

3   *Strive for incremental change* – Embrace the concept of gradual change, or change over time, by building into your design strategy a feedback loop that initiates further design and provides payback. Incremental design allows you to design a little at a time. There will never be a time when the system is perfectly designed. It will always be subject to change in the future – though that future may be beyond the bounds of your immediate project.

4   *Travel light* – The design strategy should produce no "extra" design. There should be enough to suit the current purposes (the need to do quality work), but no more.

If you embrace change, you will be willing to start simple and continually refine. The design of e-learning courses is one of incremental change. Academic studies of online course development talk about this need for incremental change when addressing the typical lifecycle of development and maintenance.

- After the first course delivery, typically 20–30 percent of the course is changed based on instructor and student feedback.
- Following the second or third delivery, another 10–15 percent of the course is changed based on student and instructor experience.
- Subsequent changes tend to occur due to technology upgrades, current events that impact topical content, changes in experiential expectations of students, or sometimes the designer or developer learns a better way to work or to present learning opportunities that were not previously available.

In the higher education environment, courses are sometimes offered only once or twice a year, and sometimes even less often. In those cases, this change may happen over two or three years. The bottom line is: No matter how well designed the course is, it will need to be changed once it is delivered and you receive feedback. This argues even more for simple, quality design that meets the objectives but no more.

Course templates

So how do you keep the design simple and hold down costs and time, while still delivering a quality product? One way is to use course templates for content, activities, assessment, and any part of the delivery mechanism that is consistent from one lesson to the next or from one course to the next.

Course templates can make a huge difference in both speeding up the design and development process, as well as providing a consistent framework for the student. Templates identify the look and feel throughout the course (e.g., font sizes, header sizes, colors, image placement) – usually with a style sheet environment. They also provide a consistent layout of activities and interactions. For example, you may choose to begin every lesson with an icebreaker activity, followed by assigned readings and a discussion. By providing an order to the activities, these templates not only help developers to concentrate on the content, but they also help the students to easily navigate the course and to know what the expectations are from one lesson to the next.

An effective, well-designed, online course contains:

- comprehensive orientation and syllabus documents with explicit student expectations;
- consistent and complete course chunks/module structure;
- redundant and consistent instructional cues and detailed explanations;
- meaningful and consistent course section and document titles to organize and convey information about the activities, content, and structure of the course;
- a detailed orientation for each course module;
- detailed instructions for each learning activity, i.e., expectation, timeframe, navigation, etc.;
- course information that is accessible and redundant;
- ample opportunities for interaction with the instructor and with others in the course; and
- opportunities to engage and interact with the content actively – directed-learning activities.

Let's look at several different examples of how you might approach template design. The first step is to determine the primary structure you wish to use in your e-learning courses. Many academic institutions select a weekly structure because it keeps students on task. The template is then developed to reflect the types of activities that may be available with each week. Figure 4.3 provides a diagram from Florida State University describing how they structure weekly course templates to include reading assignments, presentations, assessments,

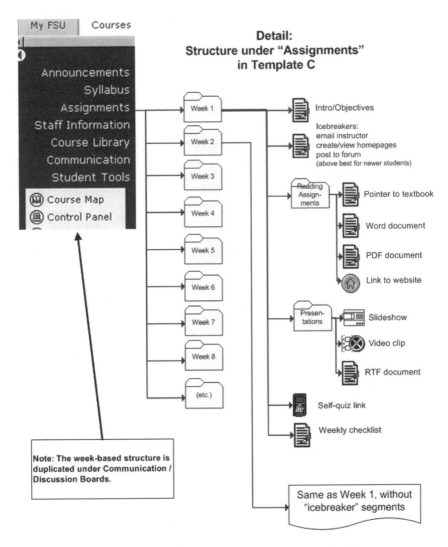

Figure 4.3 Course structure templates.

Source: Joseph Clark, Florida State University. Used by permission.

and a checklist. The only week that deviates at all from this structure is the first week, where an introductory description and icebreaker activity are also added.

Once you have a structure down, you then determine what type of navigation you wish to provide for your students. This is often referred to as the navigational template. Some projects may decide to rely completely on the inherent navigation within a learning management system. Most systems provide general navigation to items such as course content, communication tools, assessments, etc. Other projects may decide to add an internal level of navigation to these general items, as well as to more specific sub-items. Yet, other projects may decide to develop a unique navigation system that best meets the needs of their topics, students, and instructors. Let's look at three different approaches to navigational templates that provide alternatives to the simple navigation built in to most learning management systems.

An icon-driven template has been popular for the past decade. In the example below, from Portland State University, the designers decided to use icons to

Figure 4.4 Icon-driven navigational template.

Source: Misty Hamideh, Portland State University. Used by permission.

navigate both content and communication tools. The "contextos" are the weekly lessons. The decision for this choice was one that involved catering to students' visual memory for navigation instead of word memory. In later Spanish courses the icons are used with the Spanish names instead of the English names.

Icons may be used as the sole navigation or in conjunction with the typical learning management system navigation as a left bar.

In the next example, Figure 4.5, designer Virgil Varvel, at the University of Illinois, decided to combine the linear navigation available in the learning management system with a pictorial navigation representing the relationships of themes and content to the metaphor of real-world practice of copyright and intellectual property law. This navigational template is one that allows learners to approach the course in a number of different ways.

Activity templates

Once the navigation template is determined, the template (or multiple templates) for the internal lessons are the next step. Again, depending on the topic, students, faculty, and time and budget constraints these templates may be simple or complex.

In Figure 4.6, from Gail Wortmann, Bryan Bauer, Dave Carson, and Paula Yalpani at Iowa Public Television (IPTV), the internal modular design is one that provides a great deal of complexity by providing access to all materials needed for this particular lesson on the opening page of the lesson. Though the template is complex, the design is clear and simple to follow. The student knows the learning goals, what is expected in terms of active learning and participation, and how to access all the lesson materials needed to complete the required activities. In addition, the "special instructions" area at the bottom of the page draws the students' attention to any unique requirements for this particular unit and prepares them for a future unit.

Pedagogical considerations of template use in the design process

E-learning systems are often dedicated to only one delivery method – that of a linear, scaffolded approach using primarily text-based content with a few graphics and an occasional discussion. Contrast that with the variability of a good traditional classroom, where students interact in small groups, ask and answer questions, engage in real-life simulation or practice, and may make presentations demonstrating their knowledge in the topic.

As discussed in Chapter 1, the ultimate goal would be to develop systems with varied pedagogical methods where the student can choose between different methods according to the learning strategy best for him or her. Of course, the

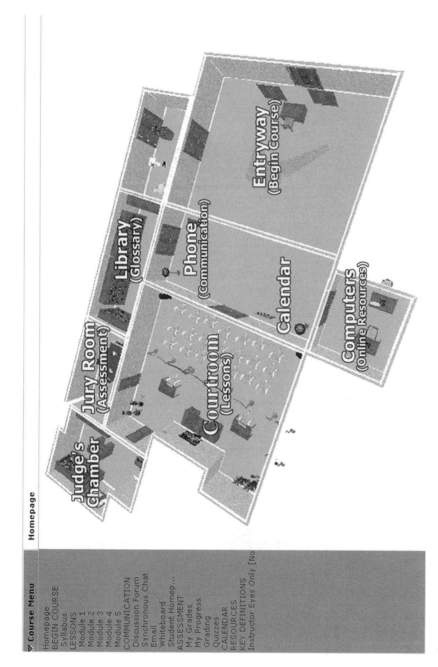

Figure 4.5 Metaphorical navigational template.

Source: Virgil Varvel, University of Illinois. Used by permission.

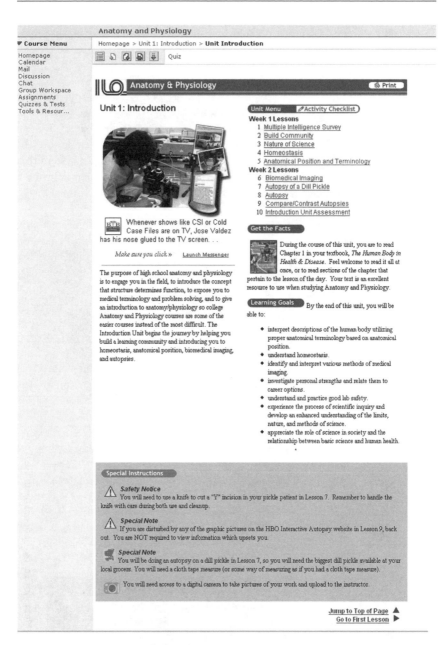

Figure 4.6 Complex template with clear design.

Source: Gail Wortmann, Bryan Bauer, Dave Carson, Paula Yalpani, at Iowa Public Television. Used by permission.

expense of this goal makes it unreachable. However, there are ways to approach this goal by using a design process that is more efficient and effective by creating tools that simplify the process for the various design stakeholders (i.e., instructors, instructional designers, and managers).

The key is to plan and use some development time in building a flexible system that allows for a variety in input to then create an output meeting the template needs described above. One way to do this is to determine "design patterns" that exist within your population's curriculum needs. Design patterns are archetypes based on well-used solutions. They build on the expertise of experienced instructors and online designers. An input system that allows you to describe a problem that occurs frequently, and then describe a solution to that problem would certainly provide a unique systematic design process.

Kolas and Staupe (2006), at the Norwegian University of Science and Technology, have begun designing interactive development templates based on such "design patterns." In the early stages of their work, they have defined five pedagogical patterns that have solutions associated with them and they are now tying these patterns to specific templates (see Figure 4.7) that provide a systematic means for generating production courses.

You might approach this problem by creating templates for each of these pedagogical patterns and providing a choice as to how each of these problems are resolved in the online environment. For example, problem-solving patterns may be implemented via case studies represented in static Web pages associated with assignments to interact on a discussion board or in a Web-conference. Depending on the topic and instance within the course, the resolution is varied and it may be that each resolution type needs a template as well. You want the student to have a similar experience every time a problem-solving opportunity is presented and to know immediately the variety of approaches that may be used to tackle that learning task.

The key is keeping the overarching look and feel of your templates similar, so that only the implementation differs. By using this approach you may come closer to meeting the varied needs of your students, while providing an equivalent or better experience than might be achieved in a traditional classroom environment.

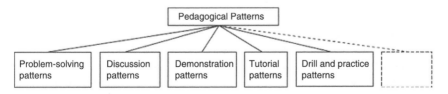

Figure 4.7 Pedagogical patterns matched to associated templates.

Rapid e-learning design and development (rapid prototyping)

Rapid e-learning development is a hot topic among many workplace learning and development practitioners. Traditional development methods involve using subject matter experts (SMEs) to pass on information to the instructional designer who, in turn, designs the solution. A developer then builds the interactive solution based on this design, and the quality assurance team tests the solution against the design and test plan. This waterfall approach can lead to long and costly design and development cycles, which can reduce the effectiveness of material with critical timelines or content that is constantly changing.

According to some estimates, the cost for traditional e-learning solutions can range between US$10,000 and $50,000 per hour of e-learning – a cost that may be prohibitive to many organizations. Traditional online courseware development timelines are measured in terms of months or years, whereas rapid e-learning timelines are measured in terms of days and weeks. This makes it an attractive solution for many institutions. Rapid e-learning development uses tools and processes that may decrease development time dramatically.

As the popularity of rapid e-learning grows, the number of development tools increases. Tools on the market include:

- Web-conferencing (Acrobat Connect, Horizon Wimba, Elluminate, WebEx);
- image and process capturing (Captivate, Articulate Presenter);
- authoring tools which create interactive modules or entire courses by generating the code needed (usually XML or Flash); these tools include: Lersus, Content Point, Mindflash, Macromedia Authorware and Director, as well as up to 50 other similar tools;
- survey and assessment tools ranging from linked free online surveys to complex and high cost testing tools;
- study and drill and practice tools (Hot Potatoes, Respondus Study Mate).

These tools leverage common business tools and automate applications to accelerate and simplify the development process. This also means that editing and updating content can be done quickly and painlessly.

For example, consider Acrobat Connect – originally called Express Trainer, then Macromedia Breeze before Adobe bought it. Similar to other web-conferencing tools, Acrobat Connect uses PowerPoint as its main development agent. In addition, Acrobat Connect also offers the benefit of easily adding an audio track to the courseware. Using a standard computer microphone, the developer can add the audio component while sitting at their desk, saving the time and cost of traditional audio recording sessions and manipulation. Other features of web conferencing include assessment and tracking and are

AICC- and SCORM-compliant. By publishing out to Flash, the courseware is presented to the learner in a user-friendly medium that is available on 98 percent of all browsers. Acrobat Connect also uses XML tags, which enables content to be indexed and fully searchable.

Process changes

In addition to using tools to help shorten the duration of development time, some advocates of rapid e-learning development also propose a change to the design process. Some organizations have their SMEs develop the content and work directly with these rapid e-learning tools to design the courseware. This process can work very well for content management. It does not work as well where more complex instructional design is critical. Furthermore, many SMEs – such as university faculty or K-12 teachers – have neither the time nor inclination to learn these tools and the design process. This is where the use of templates provides a solution to SME development.

The prototype development process is another situation where rapid e-learning tools can add value. Typically, the prototype phase can be a very costly and frustrating phase of development because the client needs to approve the design specification before implementation. Unfortunately, many clients are uncertain of their requirements at the beginning of the design process and continue to ask for changes to the prototype in the early phases. This leads to a costly and time-consuming iterative cycle in which developers must continually tweak the prototype code.

By using rapid e-learning development tools, a true prototype that represents an actual vertical slice of the courseware early in the design cycle is possible. By being able to develop this quickly and inexpensively, courseware designers/ developers can get feedback not only from the sponsor, but also from representatives of the end user group. This allows the feedback on the design, language, and metaphors from the end users, to be integrated into the design cycle early in the process when it is most useful and least expensive to make changes.

Rapid e-learning development is most useful for low- to mid-range levels of e-learning complexity in which knowledge and comprehension is key. It's typically considered less effective for high-end solutions in which evaluation and synthesis are critical. However, many rapid e-learning development tools have the capacity to embed more engaging and rich media for projects that may need a blended solution. This easy interoperability increases the versatility of the product. Also, as rapid e-learning development continues to grow in popularity, additional tools will be available to the market.

How roles change as the project matures

At the beginning of the project, through the planning and initiation phases, the project manager is more like a dictator. All documents and control are developed and maintained by him or her. The management strategy tends to be centralized and controlled. This is necessary in the beginning of the project to ensure a completed plan is developed and all stakeholders agree to the plan.

At the executing stage, however, the management strategy needs to evolve in order for the project to continue on a rapid timeline. Also, at this stage, the project has grown to such a size that one person can't manage everything and stay on schedule.

On the one hand, the project manager may wish to make all the decisions. There is no communication overhead because there is only one person responsible to upper management. There is only one person with the vision and the need to know everything about the project. Unfortunately, this strategy doesn't work, because no one person knows enough to do a good job of making all the decisions. Management strategies that are balanced toward centralized control are also difficult to execute, because they require lots of overhead on the part of those being managed.

On the other hand, the opposite strategy doesn't work either. You can't just let everyone go off and do what they want without any oversight. People inevitably go off on tangents. Someone needs to have a bigger view of the project, and to be able to influence the project when it gets off course. So, once again, we can fall back on principles to help us navigate between these two extremes.

1   *Accept responsibility.* It is the project manager's job to highlight what needs to be done, not to assign work.
2   *Ask for quality work.* The relationship between the project managers, product managers, and the designers/developers needs to be based on trust – trust that everyone wants to do a good job. The manager's role in this becomes not overseeing the work, as much as providing the tools and means for quality work to get done.
3   *Encourage incremental change.* The project manager provides guidance along the way based on feedback from all stakeholders and workers, not a big policy manual at the beginning.
4   *Embrace local adaptations.* Be aware of how the requirement to develop immediate and flexible products clashes with the organizational culture for slow and deliberate development, and find a way to resolve the misfit.
5   *Keep meetings to a minimum.* As the project matures meetings should actually decrease. Meetings impose a lot of overhead – in particular long, all-hands meetings, lengthy status reports, constant paperwork. Whatever is required to keep everyone informed shouldn't take much time to fulfill. During the execution phase everyone should be executing, not always reporting.
6   *Employ honest measurements.* Whatever metrics you use to gather feedback data should be at realistic levels of accuracy. Don't try to account for every second of work, or even minutes of work. Imagine that your watch

can only calculate to the nearest hour, or even day. Otherwise, workers in the execution phase will most likely inflate the hours in order to cover themselves.

The strategy that emerges from this phase is one of decentralized decision-making rather than centralized control. The project manager's job is to keep everyone on task, to collect metrics, to make sure the assessment is seen by those whose work is being measured, and occasionally to intervene in situations that can't be resolved in a distributed way.

A part of the project manager's job, and often the job of other leaders on the team, is to be a good coach. Good coaches are effective at getting a player to work well at their position. They spot deviations from the usual practice of the position and either help the player correct the deviation, or understand why it is acceptable for that player to do things a little differently.

However, a great coach knows that the positions are merely customary, not laws of nature. From time to time, the game changes or the players change enough so that a new position becomes possible or an old one becomes obsolete. Great coaches are always looking for what advantages could be had by creating new positions and eliminating existing ones.

Remember: the project succeeds only through collaboration. The tighter delivery schedules for most e-learning projects require an approach that demands excellent skills in collaboration and adaptation. You need to lead your team of stakeholders in ways that emphasize ongoing self-evaluation and self-regulation. Watch for early signs of "us versus them" in relationships between course designers/developers and the customer. Make sure that both parties understand the "metaphor" for the final product, its purpose, and how everyone is equally vested in its creation and success.

Chapter 5

Controlling the project

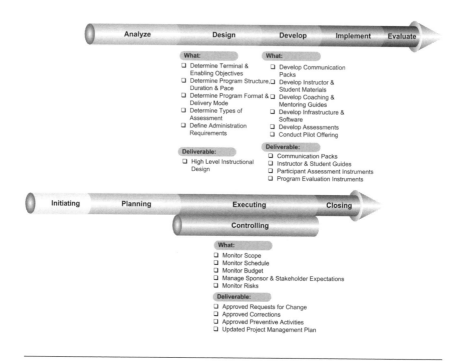

The controlling phase of the course development project overlaps with designing and developing the course. The figure at the top of this chapter illustrates the relationship of the two processes, identifies actions that are performed in each of the respective processes and the corresponding deliverables from those processes.

Results of recent studies show that slightly less than 30 percent of software development projects succeeded (were delivered on time, on budget, and with required features and functionality). What happened to the other 70 percent? Approximately 20 percent of those failed (were never delivered) while the remaining 50 percent were delivered – but either over budget and/or late – possibly with limited features and functionality. This brings us back to the concept of triple constraints introduced in Chapter 2 and illustrated again here in Figure 5.1.

Considering the results of the studies mentioned above, approximately 50 percent of the projects were delivered over budget (resources) and/or late (time) – possibly with limited features or functionality (scope). There is constant tension between the desire to add functionality and the requirement to

Figure 5.1 Triple constraints.

control time and resources while maintaining quality. During the controlling phase of the project, the project manager will collect project status information from project team members and customers. The method used is less important than being proactive in seeking information. Information collected should include progress made, percent complete, and a forecast that indicates when the activities will be completed. This is also a good time to seek input about activity dependency changes and whether activities should be added or removed from the plan. The information gathered can be interpreted to identify variances, evaluate overall project performance, and develop monthly status reports. Key areas to watch for variances are project scope, schedule, and resource utilization.

Activities that occur during this phase of course development include:

- monitoring scope (course requirements)
- monitoring the schedule (tracking progress)
- monitoring the budget
- managing sponsor and stakeholder expectations
- monitoring risk.

Inputs to the controlling phase and outputs of the phase are illustrated in Figure 5.2.

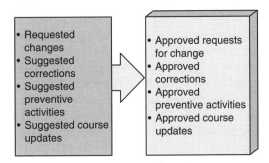

Figure 5.2 Inputs and outputs of the controlling phase of project management.

Monitoring scope

Scope creep refers to uncontrolled changes in the requirement of the course as defined in the scope definition of the project management plan. Since scope creep is a major cause of cost and time overrun, the project manager must control changes to the project charter and project scope by following the change management plan created during the planning phase of the project. Typically, increases in course scope consist of either the addition of new features to the course or a new course altogether in the case of a multi-course project. With the addition of these features or new courses, the project team may drift away from their original duties, which now might be viewed as boring since the team may be in the more mundane development stage of the project, and focus on the new course or feature, which might be viewed as exciting. To keep course development within the original cost and time estimates, the additional features or new courses must be developed within the original cost and time estimates. Since this is unlikely, the course development will go over budget or be completed late.

Sometimes changes must occur due to a change in vision, a change in the needs of the customer, even a sudden change in budget. Scope control involves trying to contain changes to project scope when that is possible and managing changes when they must occur. When scope changes are unavoidable, the project manager should identify their impact on the project plan and obtain approval from the customer and sponsor. This is accomplished by following the change control process developed during the planning phase of the project (Chapter 3). It is important to communicate any changes in timeline, budget, and risks as part of this approval process. After approval, the changes can then be communicated to project team members and stakeholders.

What are some typical changes? Changes to the course may occur when course requirements are not properly defined, documented, and controlled. Course requirements were identified during the analysis stage of ADDIE and during the initiation phase of the project. During those time periods, the project team assessed the needs of the learners, the learning environment, the product (if this course is being developed to support the use of a new product), and learning tasks. These assessments, when analyzed, identified requirements for the course that were documented in the business case for the course and locked down upon acceptance of the business case by the course sponsor and course stakeholders.

Modified or new course requirements come in two forms, additional requirements requiring unplanned work or a decrease in requirements providing a source of excess budget and/or decreased development time. Additional unplanned work may be the source of a budget overrun or late completion of the course development. Thus, changes to course requirements must be controlled through the change control process documented in the planning phase of the project and documented in the project management plan.

Monitoring the schedule (time constraint)

The next constraint that should be monitored is the time constraint. This constraint is reflected in the project schedule. The project schedule was created during the planning phase of the project and documented in the project management plan. Once the schedule is created and agreed to by the sponsor, it is considered "cast in stone." In project management terms, it is baselined. The project manager should be monitoring this baseline schedule and tracking progress against it on a regular basis.

The process for tracking this progress is recording the amount of work that has actually been performed at the activity level of the work breakdown structure and comparing that progress to the amount of work planned for that activity in the project schedule. This may be performed using the project schedule desktop application, word processor, or spreadsheet that was originally used to create the project schedule. If none of these applications was used to create the schedule, progress could be tracked using a simple list. In any case, the development schedule must be tracked to ensure that the development is proceeding as planned.

Figure 5.3 illustrates an updated Gantt chart resulting from a project team meeting that occurred on Friday, 22 July. The black bars (progress bars) included in the individual task bars indicate actual percent complete in that task. As you can see from this figure, task 11 (Develop creative briefs) has completed. The project manager has just received status reports from the work group leaders for tasks 4 (Packaging), 12 (Develop concepts), 16 (Working model), and 18 (Develop Beta List). Upon entering this into the desktop project management software and reviewing the status of these tasks against today's date, 22 July, the project manager has reason to be concerned. Task 4 is actually ahead of schedule, not a problem. However, tasks 12 and 16 are behind schedule and task 18 has not been started. As you can see from the figure, the entire Beta Test summary task, if it finishes late, will cause tasks 30 (Release to manufacturing), 31 (Manufacture product), and 32 (Project announced) to be delayed. Thus, the entire project will finish late and be categorized as a failed project! What is the project manager going to do?

Schedule control is a "balancing act" for the project manager. Initial estimates are sometimes not as accurate as we would like. Some activities are completed ahead and some behind schedule. If they are not on the critical path, they will not usually affect the overall project completion date. The project manager adjusts the plan as needed and ensures that all involved parties are informed. If the project completion or interim milestone dates are significantly shifted or delayed, he/she should obtain approval from the sponsor and the customer before they are implemented. After approval, the changes can be communicated to project team members and stakeholders.

Changes in project scope or overall schedule are sometimes extensive enough that the project manager may need to consider revisiting the planning phase

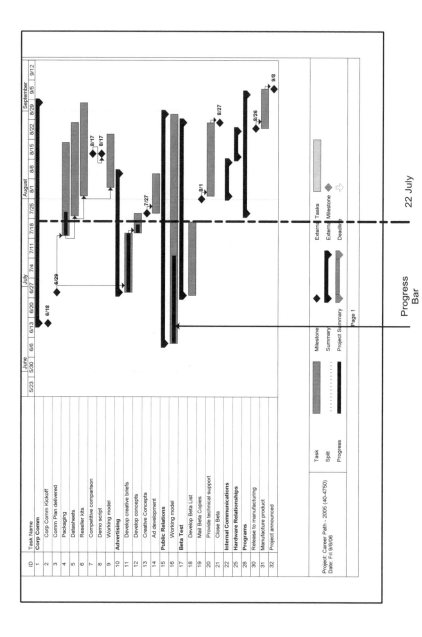

Figure 5.3 Project schedule with progress bars.

and/or updating the baseline plan. This is another area where the iterative process continues to play in the middle three phases of our process model: planning, executing, and controlling. An update to the baseline plan is not a decision to be taken lightly, however, because this may alter a historical record that could be useful when assessing project performance in the closing phase of the project.

Monitoring and controlling resources is another area that can cause changes to occur during this phase and definite restraints on time. Resource control involves assessing both how they are being utilized and in the case of human resources, whether they are able to devote the time needed to complete their activities on time. It is a rare occurrence in our environment that a resource is devoted 100 percent to a given project. When they are shared between projects, one or all of those projects can slip depending on how human resources are managed. The project manager should stay on top of this situation, while being sensitive to the other commitments of project team members. The project manager may have to escalate the issue if his or her project is being constrained by another project of similar priority.

Monitoring the schedule on a regular basis will allow corrections to be applied if the development is exceeding the plan. Corrective actions that might be applied are:

- add additional resources (people or equipment) to an activity
- start independent activities earlier
- approve overtime for personnel
- decrease the scope of the project.

Unfortunately, many of these techniques affect the constraints of resources and/or scope in Figure 5.1.

ADDIE role in the controlling phase of project management

As mentioned previously, the executing and controlling phases of project management have a great deal of overlap. The ADDIE model in design and development also overlaps during this stage. However, it is in monitoring and control of the project that the ADDIE development phase becomes most querulous.

The ADDIE development phase calls for a prototype, a tabletop review, and a pilot session. However, it's tempting to cut corners and race through the development process. This is where the project manager must carefully monitor and control this part of the ADDIE process. We live in a world where rapid prototyping and just-in-time delivery have become commonplace practices. The key is to understand how the instructional design model meshes with rapid delivery. It is not that designers can skip development steps. Rather, the steps are performed in a simultaneous and iterative process instead of a linear one.

Production and quality assurance

There are four steps (illustrated in Table 5.1) in the training development process. However, only one of these steps involves content writing. The other three steps serve as review checkpoints.

It is the role of the project manager to ensure that each of these steps is completed thoughtfully and carefully, even when time and budget seem to suggest that omitting one or more of the quality assurance steps might be acceptable.

Choices that organizations make

Why would some organizations skip these quality assurance steps during the course development process? It seems risky to launch an untested course. Learners may encounter inaccurate, incomplete, or even confusing learning materials. Table 5.2 presents the four typical reasons that an institution's course developers and project leaders make the choice to forego the quality assurance steps.

Many project leaders trust their course developers to make the right choices. However, it's important to remember that many training projects are led and created by people who are not instructional designers and thus may not be intimately familiar with the ADDIE training model or any instructional design model. After all, not every e-learning project includes an instructional designer, yet the project members have to determine how to create a course that meets their needs.

Of course, the irony is that the course developers who are unaware of the ADDIE methodology are also the people who could generally benefit the most from these quality assurance steps.

Table 5.1 Steps in training development process

Development Step	Value	Role
Prototype	Produce and review samples of content and layout	Quality assurance
Develop materials	Create all course materials	Content creation
Tabletop review	Check content for completeness and accuracy	Quality assurance
Course pilot	Measure learner's response to the materials	Quality assurance

Table 5.2 Reasons organizations choose to forego quality assurance

Reason	Effect
Don't know about instructional design processes, and specifically the ADDIE methodology.	• Course developers can become so focused on writing course content that they don't think about quality assurance. • Team members may not know how to check the course material quality.
Don't see the value of quality assurance.	• Because of time constraints, managers will not allow sufficient time for quality assurance activities in the project schedule. • Some organizations treat quality assurance steps as desirable but impractical choices for this project.
Have a limited project budget.	• The project may face a strong temptation to reduce the scope of the prototype and course pilot steps in order to meet budget constraints.
Have confidence in the course developer's skills to ensure quality in the first pass.	• A very skilled developer can possibly take informed shortcuts and still create a good course. • Without sufficient testing, increased risk will result when course is launched.

Why experience matters

An experienced instructional designer draws on lessons they've learned from past projects, and uses that knowledge throughout the design, development, and implementation processes. In the prototype phase, they don't have to reinvent the wheel. They can draw upon past prototypes, which will help them to move through this phase more quickly. During the tabletop review, instructional designers can quickly flag specific areas for special attention and prepare questions and issues to be resolved by the subject matter experts (SMEs). Finally, when they pilot a course, they are accustomed to paying attention to issues and organizing them into a comprehensive testing platform.

In short, an experienced instructional designer knows how to maximize the value of each quality assurance task. They also know how to minimize the time spent on peripheral and less important issues. Though it is tempting not to invest in an instructional designer, and it is equally tempting to forego quality assurance, we believe the risk to your e-learning program is too high to justify those decisions.

Monitoring the budget (resources constraint)

The resources constrained in Figure 5.1 include items that require funding (i.e., people, equipment, etc.) and affect the budget of the project. The budget was estimated in the initiation phase of the project and finalized in the project management plan. This budget may have been created using the desktop project management software, word processor, or spreadsheet. The project manager or financial representative for very large projects will need to track expenses against this budget to ensure that a cost overrun does not occur.

When considering the three constraints you may be able to visualize that if the scope of the course increases due to reasons discussed above, the time and resources sides of the triangle will have to lengthen to accommodate the increased scope. Thus the cost of the project will increase and the project will miss the target completion date. To ensure that the project manager is aware of the current status of the project and these three constraints, the project manager should schedule regular status meetings with the team – the authors suggest a weekly status meeting with the project team.

Issue management

Throughout the executing phase, and the monitoring/controlling phase numerous issues arise during the project. Some of these are minor, whereas others can have measurable impacts on the three constraints discussed above. How the project manager chooses to manage and document these issues is very important to the success of the project. This is particularly acute if the project has a lot of politics surrounding its success or failure.

All issues need to be identified, recorded, and communicated to those affected or concerned. Appropriate responses or counter-measures need to be developed, resourced, and deployed to ensure that all the issues within individual component projects and those relating to the overall program are managed, monitored, and controlled.

One of the ways to manage and document issues is to use an issues register (illustrated in Figure 5.4 and available on the website at http://www.routledge.com/textbooks/9780415772204), and update it regularly to all

No	Identified by	Date Raised	Issue (description)	Owner	Impact	Links to other Programmes and/or Projects	Next Actions/Current Status	Target Resolution Date	Date Closed
30									
31									
32									
33									
34									
35									
36									
37									
38									
39									
40									

Figure 5.4 Issues register (Excel file).

concerned stakeholders. The register records identified issues according to issue description and assessed impact (rated as high, medium, or low). Wherever raised, all issues need to be documented and:

- be given a unique identifier;
- described in summary terms;
- assigned an owner (someone who can manage the issue);
- rated in terms of impact (i.e., as high, medium, or low program impact);
- have a review and a target resolution date;
- have a record of status and progress.

An Action Plan or counter-measures can be identified to show the measures in place or being considered to minimize the impact. The register will also identify the timescale for resolution and/or review of the issue identified. Suitable owners for each issue need to be identified. The owners should be the person best placed to effectively and proactively manage the identified issue. New issues can be identified at all times and at all levels. All issues identified should be added to the register, even if they seem minimal and can be closed swiftly. The register provides a nice history of how the project was managed in terms of the multitude of issues.

Within a project, issues usually fall into one of three categories:

1   *Project-level issues* – problems that risk the entire program may stop the program from being delivered. An example of this might be the discovery of a major bug in the learning management system which means student knowledge assessments may not record accurately, thus impacting student grading and progress in a course or entire major curriculum.
2   *Subprogram-level issues* – problems that risk one part of the project, but not necessarily the entire project. An example of this would be a plan for single sign-on capabilities. Single sign-on allows students and instructors to sign into the organizations intranet with one login and password and automatically have that authentication passed to the learning management system and all subsequent components. If single sign-on fails to complete because of delays or bugs, it does not necessarily endanger the entire project. It certainly impacts the usability and creates other difficulties (i.e., additional training or instructional materials may need to be developed to explain a dual sign on and password environment), but the primary project can still continue.
3   *Organizational-level issues* – problems that impact the organizational structure or day-to-day operations. The issue of resources mentioned earlier is an organizational one. Other organizational issues that often cause problems are a change in the executive management, causing sponsorship to be in jeopardy; or a change in stakeholder support in one of the subgroups (i.e., faculty) that may create delivery problems.

It is important to note that both organizational- and subprogram-level issues may well escalate to become project-level issues if the issues are not resolved or become so problematic that they threaten the success of the project delivery.

Managing sponsor and stakeholder expectations

The communication management plan, developed in the planning phase of the project (Chapter 3), identified key stakeholder issues and preferences for communication by stakeholders. Following the communication plan when addressing issues is key to managing sponsor and stakeholder expectations. In the authors' most recent project, the executive sponsor is engaged in the entire project process and development stages. He attends all project meetings and actively participates in all decisions. However, in most instances, the executive sponsor is not this involved and not a member of the project team so must be apprised of the status of the project. The project team is most likely meeting on a regular basis – we recommend weekly – to provide progress reports, task status, and issues. The communication plan may be referenced as issues are raised to identify stakeholders who need to be informed of the issue. Additionally, this plan identifies their communication preferences. If new issues arise that were not identified during the planning phase of the project, the communication plan may be used to categorize the issue and identify which stakeholders will be concerned. In addition, the communication plan identifies communication preferences for the affected stakeholder. Any changes to the scope of the project, the agreed delivery date (schedule), the agreed budget (resources), and changes to the agreed quality must be communicated to the sponsor. These are potential changes to the contract, project charter, with the sponsor. As you may know from your own personal experiences, alerting the sponsor and stakeholders to potential changes in the project is preferable to having them become aware of the changes when they become a major problem. This is another example of the iterative nature of the planning, executing, and controlling phases of the project. Stakeholder communication is of the utmost importance.

Monitoring risk

Along with the identification of potential scope creep, resource constraints, and issue identification, the weekly status meeting is a time to review the risk management plan completed during the planning phase of the project. This worksheet identified potential risks, their probability of occurrence, their impact on the project, and a proposed response for the risk. This review of the risk management plan should be performed to:

1 Check to see if potential risks did occur.
2 Respond to those risks that did occur.
3 Identify new potential risks.

Initial risk management plans, like all project plans, are never perfect. One consequence of accepting changes to the agreed course requirements and project scope is the creation of new, previously unidentified risks. Planning for these risks should follow the same process and procedures as those executed in the planning phase (Chapter 3). Once identified, the potential risk should be assessed to determine the probability of occurrence, impact on the project task, and proposed response following the process outlined in Chapter 3. The importance of risk identification, response planning, and monitoring cannot be trivialized. Entire consultancies have been created just to handle project risks. However, this process cannot be allowed to assume too high priority – the results of this could keep an organization from ever completing a project!

As you have seen during this chapter, weekly project status meetings are the source of crucial project information. Project managers will either receive a tremendous amount of information or virtually no information. The amount of information and nature of that information is determined by how the project manager runs the status meeting.

In addition to professional project management competencies, project managers must possess interpersonal (soft skills) and leadership skills. Many topics included in this chapter have highlighted the need for soft skill competence (e.g., listening, oral and written communication, problem-solving, acquisition and evaluation of information, and negotiation to arrive at a decision) as well as leadership skill competence (e.g., influence, coach team members, and partner with teams). Project team members must feel open to bring any concern to the project team and believe that they and the concern will be treated with respect and, if needed, confidentiality. The project team must be a safe haven for project team members.

The project manager walks a fine line here – being open to requests for change, concerns, potential risks to project completion, etc., while leading the team to the agreed requirements contained in the project charter. Many project managers have ruled with an iron fist and run troubled projects.

Project plans used during the controlling phase

Actually, considering the iterative nature of the project management planning, executing and controlling phases, it would appear that those were the only phases where project control occurs. However, actually controlling the project occurs in all phases. The project team may refer to documents and plans developed in each project phase to guide them as they control the project. Table 5.3 is a guide to project management documents available during each project phase.

Table 5.3 Plans by project phase

Project Management Phase	Documents and Plans
Planning	Project management plan, including: • scope definition • work breakdown structure • risk management plan • change management plan • schedule • budget • staffing • communication management plan • procurement plan
Executing	Request for change Approved requests for change Approved preventive activities Approved course updates
Controlling	Request for change Approved requests for change Approved corrections Approved course updates Updated project management plan Updated project scope statement

Formative evaluation and evolutionary design

As mentioned in Chapter 4, formative evaluation is performed during the development of the course. In evolutionary design, the development of the course is divided into subsets of the course – possibly prototypes of the course (see Figure 5.5).

In this instance, the development of the course has been subdivided into three prototypes and the final course. At the end of each of these development stages, a usability study, formative evaluation, will be performed to evaluate course navigation, course contents for that prototype, objective attainment, etc. Analysis of the results of the formative evaluation provides input to the design stage of the next prototype.

Each prototype might be a course module or possibly might test course navigation, assessment techniques, techniques for remote communication, etc. Techniques to perform the formative evaluation might be a survey (questionnaire), possibly administered over the Internet or sent as an e-mail attachment, an observation form administered in person, or free notes gathered in a word processor and delivered via e-mail.

When all evaluations have been collected, analysis of those evaluations is performed to determine the result (e.g., course navigation is poor and needs to

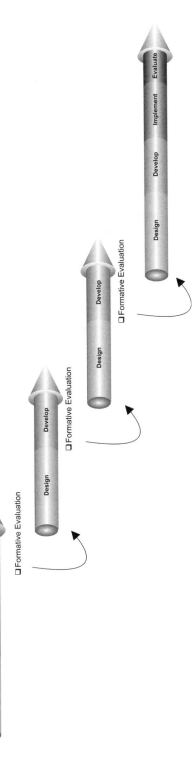

Figure 5.5 Evolutionary design using formative evaluations.

be redesigned, course module 1 did not meet its terminal objectives and needs to be redesigned, course module 1 met all terminal objectives – design and develop module 2, etc.). These results are the input to the next design-development stage of the evolutionary design. The cycle of design-develop-formative evaluation continues until the whole course is developed and evaluated. Then it's on to the implementation and evaluation stages of ADDIE.

Summary of the controlling phase

The controlling phase of the project is an overarching phase of the project. In many projects the controlling phase causes iterations of the planning and execution phases of the project as changes are requested and approved that require updates to existing plans in the project management plan. Scope creep, uncontrolled changes to the project, is the result of:

*   poor change control;
*   lack of proper identification of which products and features are required to complete the course development;
*   a weak project manager or executive sponsor.

The controlling phase of the project relies predominately on the request for change process as documented in the change management plan of the project management plan to control project scope creep. During the executing phase of the project (Chapter 4 of this text), this project management plan is executed to design, develop, and deliver the e-learning project.

Chapter 6

Closing the project

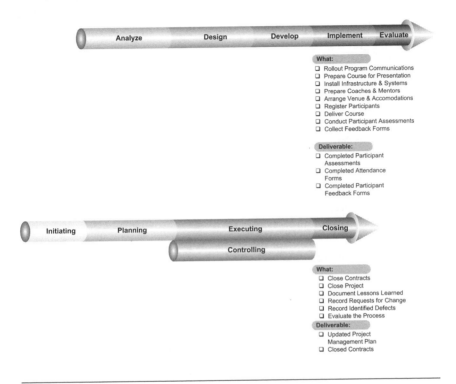

The closing phase of the course development project overlaps with implementing the course. The figure at the top of this chapter illustrates the relationship of the two processes, identifies actions that are performed in each of the respective processes and the corresponding deliverables from those processes. The closing phase of the project is the most likely of the phases to be overlooked by the project manager and the project team. For all purposes, the project has completed! The course has been turned over to the owner and is being scheduled and delivered. However, there is still valuable work to be done.

Just as in all relationships, closure is important. In project management the project requires closure after achieving its objectives or being terminated for other reasons. Closing the project not only provides for completion of administrative activities, but also provides evaluation of project performance which can be a valuable learning tool for the project manager as well as others.

The project plan, baseline plan, and other project records have been compiled and updated throughout the project's life. Project facts or statistics should be compiled from project information that will assist in the assessment of project performance. These might include comparisons of the baseline plan to project plan, plan to actual results, scope changes, milestones to actual results, and others. This, plus information about the delivered product, will be used to assess project performance.

Let's look more specifically at the sets of activities which must occur during the closing phase of the project.

1   Hand off to the implementing organization.
2   Ensure project deliverables meet stakeholder requirements.
3   Close the project:

    i   close contracts;
    ii   document lessons learned during the project.

4   Release resources.
5   Evaluate the project process.

Steps 1 through 4 above formally complete the project and clearly end the project to the sponsor and all stakeholders. It is important to secure this agreement to indicate to the sponsor and stakeholders that any additional work will require a new project and project team.

Hand-off to the implementing organization

During the planning phase of the project, the project team identified activities for the hand-off of the e-learning project to the implementing organization. These activities may have included the development and delivery of the following:

- the development of customer service procedures documented in a manual, a help system, and frequently asked questions document;
- the development of administrative procedures documented in a manual, a help system, and frequently asked questions document;
- the development of information technology/information services procedures documented in a manual, help system, and frequently asked questions document;
- the development of end user procedures documented in a manual, help system, and frequently asked questions document;
- a training course for customer service, administrative, and end users.

These items were all designed and developed in the executing and controlling phases of the project and delivered to the respective users in the closing phase of the project. When these documents, procedures, and help systems and the relevant training have been transferred and delivered, the staff in the respective organizations are prepared to implement the e-learning project.

Obtain agreement on deliverables

During the design and development phases of this e-learning project, your relationship with the sponsor and major stakeholders may have been strained. It is quite likely that they wanted enhancements to the original scope of the project as described in the project charter. And, considering the ever-present concerns regarding the project's triple constraints, you were not eager to agree to those enhancements. So, here we are at the end of the project, and you must secure agreement from the sponsor that the project is finished. Hopefully, in spite of the difficulties and challenges you may have faced during the project, your relationship with the sponsor and key stakeholders is still amicable.

The project deliverables, as modified through the change management process, have been completed, tested, and transferred to the organization responsible for on-going operation. Now is the time to signal to the sponsor and key stakeholders that the project is finished. Any new updates, enhancements, fixes, etc. are outside of the scope of this project. A new project with new funding and a new team must be chartered for those enhancements.

The best way to signal the finality of this activity is to obtain the sponsor's signature, possibly on the project charter, agreeing to the completion. Now that the sponsor has agreed that the project is finished, it's time to close all contracts with internal and external consultants and vendors and to store lessons learned into a knowledge base.

Project closure report

As with any other project decisions, authority to close or merge a project should be carefully documented. The most effective way of doing this is by production of a project closure report. This should document the following:

- reasons for closure;
- who authorized closure and the agreement or sign-off from the project board and/or sponsor;
- date of the decision;
- timescale for closure (a revised project plan or exit strategy, showing the timescale for controlled shutdown of the project, including all its constituent parts, unless they have been transferred or handed over to other projects or operations);
- statement of delivery against the project plan. This should record if all the deliverables are on time, cost and quality standards (any slippage should be noted);

- how residual risks are to be managed (i.e., by whom);
- how residual issues to be handled (i.e., by whom and by when);
- how internal and external communications are to be handled;
- how project resource issues are to be handled (e.g., handling of staff/HR issues, remaining budget funds or liabilities);
- transfer of responsibilities for the delivery of still required deliverables or outcomes (To whom? Are the target dates different?);
- confirmation of whether lessons learned have been captured and reported;
- how the post-closure evaluation (in the form of post-implementation review) is to be conducted (by whom, by when, and how resourced);
- confirmation that project documents have been completed and scrubbed of any superfluous material in line with institutional records management guidance. Also that they have been closed and archived or handed over to the team responsible for managing any residual or operational issues and risks.

This project closure report is generated from the steps and processes indicated in the remainder of this chapter.

Close the project

To close the project, the project manager must verify that all project contracts originated for the project have been closed and the deliverables have been delivered to and accepted by the sponsor and receiving organization. All project records should be reviewed to determine the success or failure of that particular activity and documented to be archived as lessons learned from this project. The project management plan should be reviewed to ensure that all updates to relevant plans have been completed.

Close contracts

Just as when securing the final sign-off from the project sponsor, the project team must close all contracts with internal and external consultants and vendors. When you secured the sponsor's signature, the sponsor agreed that the deliverables met the requirements of the project. This final sign-off must also be done with internal and external consultants and vendors. Ideally, as each service was performed or each item was received, the service or item was checked to ensure that the requirements of the contract were met. However, whether or not that check was performed, now the check must be performed. You are about to sign the contract and quite possibly make the final payment for the service or goods, so that final check must be made by the project manager or project team member responsible for securing the consultant or goods.

Closing contracts includes ensuring that the contracted goods and services were acceptable and met the requirements of the contract. If the contracted resource was personnel, the project manager should ensure that the contracted personnel met requirements of the contract. In either instance, records should be updated to reflect satisfaction with the contractor since this vendor might be considered for subsequent contracts. Projects are temporary in nature, if the product or service is required for the on-going operation of the project, a new contract with the vendor must be agreed to by the implementing organization.

Post-project review – document lessons learned

Lessons learned during this project are an important knowledge base for the organization. Other projects within the organization as well as projects in external organizations will follow or adapt the best practices created during this project. The data stored as lessons learned might be the entire project management plan, techniques used to estimate activity duration and cost, satisfaction reports with contractors, satisfaction reports with vendors, potential risks to the project, and results of implemented responses to risks. All of these may be reviewed as part of the post-project review.

The objective of the review is to bring closure to the project, review project performance, identify open issues, and document lessons learned. The review should be brief and include primary project stakeholders. It is recommended that a facilitator be used during the review to guide the process of project performance assessment. Lessons learned from the project will be discovered in the review by discussing problem areas, identifying probable causes, and developing suggestions for improvement. Documentation of the post project review should be stored in an accessible place so that subsequent projects may learn from this one. Process improvement suggestions should be referred to the planning and leadership team.

Additional information will likely be collected as feedback from the post-project review which may require follow-up by the project manager. Documents should be updated to include new information. This will be especially true of the "lessons learned" document, as customers and other stakeholders may have suggestions that will be very helpful to the project manager and other projects.

The project manager should review the project records to determine the value of specific records for future projects and for historical understanding of project activities should the need arise. Records of no value should be discarded. Product documentation should be turned over to the product owner or support team. The remaining records should be moved to the project archives for future reference. A similar process should occur for hard-copy documents.

In many instances, these records are considered intellectual property and not for release outside of the organization. In other instances, these records are considered public domain and used to expand the knowledge base of the profession. In either case, the project team is relieved to have the project completed and excited to get on with the next activity on their plate.

Documenting lessons learned is often overlooked – allowing all the knowledge gained through the execution of this project to be lost to those outside of the project team. Consulting organizations, in particular, value this information, treat it as intellectual property, parse the data and plans into small reusable packages, and store these in a knowledge base.

Techniques used to store the data are:

- a simple folder system available to all employees of the organization;
- an online forum, similar to a discussion forum, with a file store for the documents and a discussion area for an on-going "conversation" with hints, tricks, and application notes for the tools and templates stored in the file store;
- a knowledge-base system that contains a data store as well as an intelligent search engine.

Of primary importance here is the actual capturing of the knowledge! As mentioned above, this step is frequently overlooked to the detriment of all subsequent projects that may have benefited from the knowledge gained in this project.

Celebrate the accomplishment – party hearty!

The course is deployed, the project is finished. The project manager has a few final activities to complete. One of the most important of these is to celebrate the accomplishment before the team is dispersed. This team has been together for quite some time. They most likely have stormed a bit and formed into a cohesive team. It may very well be that the team has spent more time together than they did with their families. Most likely, this team will never be together again. There will be new players on the next project and other team members will have moved on to new positions within the organization. Now is the time to celebrate the accomplishments, relish the good times, lightly review the bad times with their successful corrections, and just have a great time.

The authors would suggest celebrating in a private room at a very nice restaurant. However, the celebration must meet the norms of the organization. But do remember to celebrate. The question here might be "When do I schedule and how do I fund this hearty party?" We agree this is an issue! We suggest that you include the party in the project schedule.

This is an issue in the author's current project. We have met a major milestone and would like to celebrate. But there is no free time in people's schedules to allow for this celebration! Additionally, if you include the closing celebration in the project schedule, you could assign not only resources but also costs to the activity. Thus the party is funded and scheduled in all participants' calendars.

Release resources

Now that final agreements have been received from the project sponsor, all contracts with internal and external consultants and vendors have been closed, and lessons learned have been captured in the knowledge base, the staff can be released to their parent organizations. Staff records for personnel assigned to the project should be updated to reflect actual work performed. In many instances, the project manager will need to evaluate each staff member's performance. In a matrixed organization, reviews of employees by the supervisors and peers on the project teams are a significant portion of the staff member's mid-year or annual performance review. Once a formal review between the project manager and the project team member has been completed, the proper evaluation forms may be updated, results agreed, and forwarded to the parent organization for inclusion in the mid-year or annual performance review.

Additional final activities will include the disposal of physical resources that may have been acquired. Some projects may have required special tools, equipment, software, furniture, etc., that will need to be disposed of or formally transferred to another team or project. Each item should be identified and taken care of in an appropriate manner.

Evaluate the project process

Designing and developing an e-learning project by following a combined ADDIE/IPECC process may be new to the organization. Obtaining project team member, stakeholder, and sponsor perspectives regarding this combined set of processes should be recorded and evaluated. Data should be collected from these groups and analyzed for improvements to the process. Methods used to collect this data are:

- individual interviews using a form to facilitate capturing consistent information from each member;
- a panel discussion with each group using a form to capture consistent information from each group;
- an online survey.

Once the perspectives have been captured using the methods outlined above, the results should be analyzed to identify areas of improvement. These improvements may be stored in the knowledge base to make them available to project teams that follow.

Updates after project deployment

During the implementation stage of ADDIE, among the activities that are performed are delivering the course and receiving end-of-course feedback forms, reaction evaluations, and summative evaluations as discussed in Chapter 3. In Chapter 3, we discussed the techniques that may be used to collect the data. In this chapter, the implementing organization will collect the instruments, analyze the collected data, and possibly make recommendations for updates to the course. These recommendations may be recorded using the change request form created during the planning phase of the project (Chapter 3), and filed for future reference as updates to the course are considered. Planned updates to the course may have been discussed with the course sponsor during the initiation phase of the project. The timing for these updates, unless the causes for the updates are catastrophic, will be scheduled after the payback period for the course has passed. At that time, a new project will be initiated with these change request forms and any modified business requirements as input to the new initiation phase of the new project.

Post-implementation review

The post-implementation review (PIR) generally takes place 6–12 months after the formal closure of the project. Its aim is to determine whether the project delivered the benefits and outcomes that were anticipated at the beginning of the project and outlined in the business case and project scope. For example, it might assess if the new e-learning environment has delivered the streamlining of e-learning design, better student retention or performance, or has indeed allowed for a reduction in resource requirements. Its purpose is also to make recommendations to realize or improve benefits, or counter problems that were not previously identified.

Usually the sponsor or the organizational executive is responsible for defining the terms of reference for the PIR. However, sometimes the project manager may be responsible for this as part of the follow-up contract. Consequently, the project manager would also be responsible for securing any resources required to carry out the review.

The PIR should include the following:

- achievement of expected benefits;
- unexpected benefits;
- unexpected problems;
- user reactions;
- follow-on work recommendations, together with timescales and responsibilities.

Each expected benefit is assessed for the level of its achievement so far, or any additional time needed for the benefit to materialize. Some projects may require more time before benefits are quantifiable (e.g., a degree program implementation where benefits may not be measurable for two or three years) and further assessments may need to be built into the evaluation processes. Use of the product or services may have brought unexpected side effects, beneficial or adverse. These are documented with an explanation of why these were not foreseen and what suggested actions may be required.

General comments should be obtained about how the customers feel about the project deliverables. The type of observation will depend on the type of deliverable produced by the project, but examples might be its ease of use, performance, reliability, contribution it makes to their work, and suitability for the work environment.

Suggested quality criteria for a PIR are:

- It covers all benefits mentioned in the project scope and business case.
- It describes each achievement in a tangible, measurable form.
- It makes recommendations in any case where a benefit is not fully met, a problem has been identified, or a potential extra benefit could be obtained.
- It is conducted as soon as the benefits and problems can be measured.

Evaluating the combined ADDIE–IPECC process

The final process to be performed during this closing phase of the project is to evaluate the ADDIE–IPECC process. Whether this is the completion of the first course design and development using the combined ADDIE–IPECC process or the one-hundredth, recommendations to the individual processes as well as the ADDIE–IPECC process relationship should be evaluated for improvements. The authors suggest that all organizations are learning organizations. Thus, as the organization continues to apply the process, improvements to the processes may be made and the organization's skills and abilities in these processes will mature.

Summary for closing the project

Closing the project is an important phase of the project and should not be overlooked. Valuable information is gained through the project closing process and stored in the organizational knowledge base as well as in increased knowledge and experience of the project team members. Consultants and vendors have been contracted, their services used and products received, payments made, and satisfaction measured. These contracts are closed and the information stored to benefit projects that follow. The completion of the project has been celebrated. Project team members have gained knowledge and experience and been released to their parent organizations.

The project manager can take that well-deserved time off; certainly there was not time for that during the project. And, the project manager should prepare for the next project. Projects are transient – the project manager needs to find the next activity that will expand his or her experience base. As the project is moving toward completion, the project manager should be investigating that next project. The authors believe in and practice continuous learning – project managers should do this as well!

Chapter 7

Quality management

Every project should have a quality plan. In reality, very few do. Why is it that so few project management plans include quality management, or write it so lightly that it doesn't provide enough information to make a difference? The top two reasons many project managers give for lacking or not implementing a quality management plan are:

1   It is too complicated to do a plan when the product and services haven't even been piloted.
2   The jargon of quality management is overwhelming. Differentiating between assessment and quality is difficult and confusing.

Quality definition

So what is quality? There are numerous definitions of quality:

*   "Quality is fitness for use." – J. M. Juran
*   "[Quality is] meeting or exceeding customer expectations at a cost that represents a value to them." – H. James Harrington
*   Quality should be defined as surpassing customer needs and expectations throughout the life of the product." – Howard Gitlow and Shelley Gitlow

A simple layman's definition is to make sure whatever is delivered is within the quality expectations of the organization and the project charter. The expectations of the organization are important to understand. If it is NASA building rocket control systems, the expectations are likely to be higher than if it is a small retailer building a marketing database . . . hopefully. In the case of e-learning, a quality information system should provide all the quality-relevant information to the authors of e-learning materials, to the instructors and tutors, and also to the learners.

Judging quality

From a business perspective, project quality is usually judged on the following criteria:

- Did the system meet my needs when it was delivered?
- Is it stable?

From a technical perspective, project quality is usually judged as:

- Does the system comply with corporate standards for such things as user interface, documentation, naming standards, etc.?
- Is the technology stable?
- Is the system well engineered so that it is robust and maintainable?

As you can see, the perspective of quality varies depending on who we are talking to. Generally speaking however, the "fit for purpose" aspect of quality is the one we judge. Does the deliverable do the job it was designed to do?

Project quality vs. deliverable quality

The situation above illustrates the difference between judging the deliverables and judging the project. You need to decide how much focus to put on the quality of the project against the quality of the deliverables.

- The project quality refers to things like applying proper project management practices to cost, time, resources, communication, etc. It covers managing changes within the project.
- The deliverable quality refers to the "fit for purpose" aspect mentioned earlier. It covers things like how well it meets the user's needs, and the total cost of ownership.

Quality materials used in a quality management plan

Table 7.1 provides examples of "Quality Materials" that might be used in a quality management plan.

Quality events

Table 7.2 lists quality events that typically are used to review the quality of deliverables. They tend to have a different mix of reviewing the structure and reviewing the content. In other words, they check to see if the document is "well-engineered" and/or "correct" (see definitions).

Table 7.1 Quality materials used in a quality management plan

Quality Materials	Description
Standards	Standards are instruction documents that detail how a particular aspect of the project must be undertaken. There can be no deviation from "standards" unless a formal variation process is undertaken and approval granted.
Guidelines	Unlike standards, guidelines are not compulsory. They are intended to guide a project rather than dictate how it must be undertaken. Variations do not require formal approval.
Checklists	Checklists are lists that can be used as a prompt when undertaking a particular activity. They tend to be accumulated wisdom from many projects.
Templates	Templates are blank documents to be used in particular stages of a project. They will usually contain some examples and instructions. Or in the case of course development, they serve as style sheets.
Procedures	Procedures outline the steps that should be undertaken in a particular area of a project such as managing risks or managing time.
Process	A description of how something works. It is different from a procedure in that a procedure is a list of steps – the what and when. A process contains explanations of why and how.
User Guides	User guides provide the theory, principles, and detailed instructions as to how to apply the procedures to the project. They contain such information as definitions, reasons for undertaking the steps in the procedure, and roles and responsibilities. They also have example templates.
Example Documents	These are examples from prior projects that are good indicators of the type of information, and level of detail, that is required in the completed document.
Methodology	A methodology is a collection of processes, procedures, templates, and tools to guide a team through the project in a manner suitable for the organization.

Quality-relevant data in e-learning applications

To obtain a complete compilation of quality-relevant data, all the different data types occurring in the whole lifecycle of the application have to be considered. A detailed analysis of many different data types can be found within the ADDIE model we've been using throughout this book. Figure 7.1 shows only a simplified overview of the principal constituents every quality information system for e-learning applications should contain.

The quality management plan is structured according to the different phases in the lifecycle of the application.

Table 7.2 Quality events used to review deliverables

Quality Events	Description
Expert Review	Review of a deliverable by a person who is considered an expert in the area. For example, a review of a history course by a senior history professor or a known historian. The person may not currently hold a position as professor or historian, but has known expert knowledge in the area. This type of review is good when the focus is on accuracy of content (correct) rather than of structure (well engineered).
Peer Review	Peer reviews of a deliverable are better suited where the emphasis is on structure rather than content. A peer review will focus on ensuring the deliverable is well engineered. Neither an expert review nor a peer review is exclusively focused on content or structure. They each however, have a different emphasis.
Multi-person Review	Independent reviews conducted by several people are likely to pick up more points. However, multiple reviews do sometimes result in irreconcilable viewpoints. This type of review is best undertaken when the purpose is to gain agreement between different stakeholders. Time should be allowed to reach agreement of conflicting opinions.
Walk-through	A walk-through is a useful technique to validate both the content and structure of a deliverable. Material should be circulated in advance. If particular participants have not done their homework, they should be excluded from the walk-through. Too much time can be wasted bringing one person up to speed in a walk-through.
Formal Inspection	A formal inspection is a review of a deliverable by an inspector who would typically be external to the project team. In academic institutions this may be someone in the Department of Institutional Research, or an outside consultant. The inspector captures statistics on suspected defects. It is a useful technique for use with documentation.
Standard Audit	A standard audit is carried out by a person who is only focused on ensuring the deliverable meets a particular standard or standards. This type of quality control is often conducted by accrediting agencies, but there are many other quality audits that can be conducted by other internal or external reviewers.
Process Review	In this case a defined business process is reviewed to ensure all necessary actions are being undertaken, information recorded, and procedures followed. A process review is useful to validate the existing processes in an organization, and is often undertaken at the beginning of a quality management plan. Then taken again after the plan is implemented to note differences. For example, modification to an existing learning management system may be based on the assumption an existing business process is being followed. If the business process is either not being followed or is different, the modification to the LMS may have unexpected results. For a project quality check, a process review may be carried out to ensure proper change control procedures are in place. Typically someone like a project office or internal audit would complete a process review.

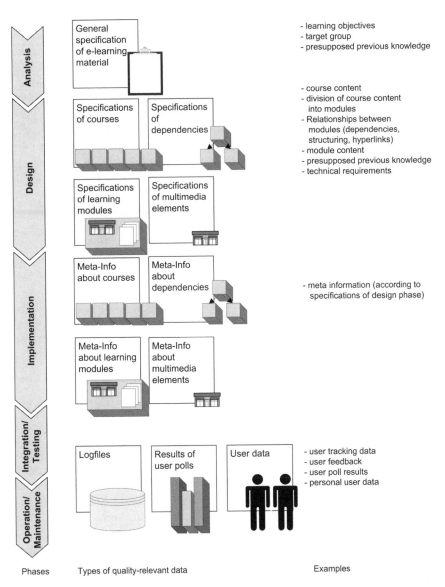

Phases   Types of quality-relevant data   Examples

Figure 7.1 Quality-relevant data.

1   In the *analysis stage* only general specifications of the planned e-learning application are generated. For example the learning objectives of the application and its target group should be defined here.

2   In the *design and development stages* the e-learning application is modeled in detail, in particular the course content and its structure has to be defined. It's very reasonable to specify all this data in a formalized way.

Then it is obviously much more adapted for automatic data-processing than the implemented e-learning content itself. In later phases this data can be used to survey whether the implemented e-learning application does suit its specifications or if it's used in a way according to them.

3   In the *implementation stage* the e-learning application has to be realized pursuant to the modeling in the preceding phases. The corresponding specifications should be transformed into the meta-information of multi-media elements, modules, and courses. Of course it makes sense to use a standard for e-learning meta-information here. If the learning modules for example are written using XML, only some special tags according to the standard have to be inserted. Remember: the learning content itself is quality-relevant of course, but it's not as accessible for automatic processing as its formalized meta-information. Therefore it's not reasonable to store the whole learning content in a quality information system.

4   In the *integration and evaluation stages*, and in the operation and maintenance stages, essentially the same types of quality-relevant data can occur. Examples for these types of data are user-tracking data, results coming from direct questionings of the users (surveys, focus groups, interviews), and personal user data including the results of learner assessments. Obviously the learners are involved in the generation of all this data and therefore their privacy has to be taken into account. For this reason all the personal data in a quality information system should be reported anonymously, or at least pseudonyms assigned for any reports.

All these types of quality-relevant data might be interesting separately, but they'll develop their significance only if they are associated with each other. If for example many users coming from the same module search for a certain word in the glossary, this might indicate that the learning module is ambiguous at a certain point. If this is not the case, some information about the learners might indicate that some knowledge the learners don't have has been presupposed in that learning module. As another example, questioning the users will become more significant if the questions are related to certain parts of the content. If these relations are specified in a formalized way, an automatic analysis will be simplified. Therefore, in any implementation of a quality information system the different types of quality-relevant data and, what is more, their relationships have to be regarded.

Developing the quality management plan

A quality plan needs to cover a number of elements:

*   Which items require a quality check?
*   What is the most appropriate way to check the quality?

- When should it be carried out?
- Who should be involved?
- What "quality materials" should be used?

Table 7.3 addresses the planning and management activities that make the project output conform to quality requirements and help to ensure a satisfied customer.

Table 7.3 Planning and management activities that meet quality requirements

	Priority Designation			
	4	*3*	*2*	*1*
Area	Quality goals easily understood, achieved, and monitored.	Quality goals can be defined and measured using existing systems and methods; quality risk low.	Quality goals are extensive, require innovative approaches; and may impact project success.	Quality goals are difficult to define; hard to measure and achieve; significant risk to project acceptance.
Quality Assurance Plan	Define quality goals; discuss approach and plans to achieve goals; assess risks to success; discuss adequacy of approach; set high standards.	Document explicit quality goals; define methods and tests to achieve, control, predict and verify success; focus on customer satisfaction.	Document QA goals, plans, methods, and systems; focus processes on minimizing correction costs.	Document QA plan including quantitative goals, statement of methods to achieve, quality metrics, controls, and verifications; link QA to stakeholder and risk analysis.
Quality Management	Consider quality management integral to project work; ensure project team understands role in achieving quality goals; have PM maintain visibility of quality issues.	Implement integrated quality management through delegated quality goals; plan work methods, technologies, measurements, and controls to achieve goals; build quality into processes and products.	Integrate quality management tasks into project plan; establish quality goals; delegate goals to work groups; report quality metrics and track progress.	Assign quality management oversight in PM staff; monitor metrics and trends to achieve quality goals; integrate quality management into project planning and risk management.

Continued overleaf

Table 7.3 continued

	Priority Designation			
	4	3	2	1
Quality Metrics, Measurements, and Controls	Conduct subjective (qualitative) or objective (quantitative) assessments periodically; monitor and report quality status at periodic project reviews.	Map quality metrics to quality goals, and report periodically; apply standard quality tools to measure, predict and control results.	Establish quality metrics and conduct quality audits to predict and verify achievement of goals and identify need for corrective actions; apply quality control techniques to project effort.	Implement best practices quality control organization; document quality methods integral to project plan; provide commitment of staff, tools, and methods to support quality effort.
Continuous Quality Improvement (CQI)	Communicate continually a project goal to work smarter and find better processes; plan the project to accommodate future improvements.	Review the project approach and design concept for modularity, expandability and growth; consider CQI in product lifecycle strategy.	Include CQI tasks in project plans and budget; establish CQI goals and metrics, and report progress periodically.	Incorporate CQI/TQM goals into specifications and plans; review project methods for improvement opportunities; institutionalize CQI processes and incorporate provisions into product design.

What needs to be checked?

Typically the items that need to be checked are the deliverables. Any significant deliverable from a project should have some form of quality check carried out. A requirements document can be considered significant. A memo or weekly report may not be significant.

For the project itself, it may be appropriate to have the project management practices reviewed for quality once the project is initially established. This may be useful to give the sponsor and steering committee a level of confidence in the team.

What is the most appropriate way to check?

To answer this question requires thinking backwards. If the end result is that a particular deliverable should meet a standard (i.e., SCORM compliance), then part of the quality checking should focus on compliance with the standard. This would indicate a "standard audit" could be the best approach.

You also need to differentiate between "correct" and "well-engineered." A well-engineered bridge course may look great, be fun for students, and not have any technical glitches. However, if it doesn't meet the learning objectives or if students are unable to pass a knowledge test as evidence of course completion, then the course is not "correct." Similarly a test plan may be clear and easy to follow but not test everything it should. Alternatively it may cover all the testing but cannot be clearly followed. Quality checking may be for either "correct" or "well engineered," or it may be for both.

When should quality checks be carried out?

Most "quality events" are held just prior to the completion of the delivery. However, if there are long development lead times for a deliverable, it might be sensible to hold earlier quality events. For example, if development of code for a particular module will take 10 weeks, it may be worth holding a code inspection after 4 weeks to identify any problems early and reduce rework.

Purchased goods and services should also be checked to ensure they meet their quality standard. This quality check is normally performed upon delivery of the goods or services.

Continuous improvement

The world is bigger than one project. What goes wrong in one project is likely to go wrong in other projects unless the cause is identified and fixed. This is particularly true in e-learning projects. If a template is missing a heading, don't just fix the project document. Fix the template. If a standard has some aspect that cannot be complied with in your environment, either change your environment or get agreement that all projects are exempt from this part of the standard. If there are no generally accepted availability criteria for business applications, don't just add some to your requirements. Get them published as organization criteria. This is what continuous improvement is all about.

Quality plan summary

Producing a quality plan is not complex. It involves identifying all the deliverables at the start of the project and deciding how best to validate their quality. There is an overhead in undertaking quality checks, but this is offset by not having to fix things further down the line. Inevitably, the later you find a problem, the longer it takes to fix.

It is also going to make your stakeholders more comfortable if they see that quality is being addressed during the project. It can even be a good public relations exercise to bring them to a quality review. Not only do they see that quality is being addressed, but it exposes them to the complexity of the project.

Finally, having uncovered the quality issues, be sure you have a mechanism in place to fix the problems. One way to do this is through the "issues tracking register" discussed in Chapter 5. This tracks the quality issue, assigns particular people to it, and provides impact and timeline details. There must be a good follow-up process to allocate fixes to particular people and ensure they actually make the changes.

Chapter 8

Change management

The simplest definition of change management is making change in a planned and managed fashion. In the context of e-learning systems, change management requires a thorough understanding of how your organization does business, how it plans to grow, and then identifying the workflows that need to change to successfully implement a new e-learning environment, or to expand (scale) an existing environment.

Even more fundamentally, it is important to understand that change management is a *political* process that requires corporate management and project managers to share their vision of how users' lives will change (presumably for the better) because of your project, and then get the users to agree to implement the changes necessary to make it work. Ultimately, change management involves people management – managing acceptance, resistance, buy-in, positive and negative experiences, and reinforcement of participation. It is the people that are the most difficult task of any project.

Entire books with hundreds of pages have been written on the topic of change management. Change management is a complex process, and there is certainly a great deal more theory and resolution than we can include in a project management book. So, this chapter will cover those areas most likely to impact e-learning systems and, in many cases, provide only the initial descriptions of how you might develop a change management plan as part of your project management responsibilities.

Role of project manager in change management

Change management in a project comes on two levels. First, and the most obvious, is during the project design and development stages. Second, and often missed, is the change management that is critical in the implementation stage. During all of these stages, change likely introduces new risks or issues which will need management. Managing change is one of the key challenges of e-learning project management and a poorly planned or executed change management environment is often one of the key reasons projects fail.

The ADDIE instructional design process dictates a type of change management process during the design and development stage of course and curriculum implementation. This is done through formative evaluation – that is evaluation of the process of design and development, followed by testing of the product. What is learned from this formative evaluation then changes the process and the product. In other words, a change management process is already in place.

However, a second critical part of your change management plan is managing the change that needs to occur for the project to succeed. This includes changing the hearts and minds of people whose daily lives will change as a result of your project.

The role of the project manager is to ensure that all requests for change are considered in a controlled manner, and that they are fully assessed in relation to their overall impact on the quality triple constraints (**Scope, Time, and Resources**). Table 8.1 defines some of the questions you might use to assess these constraints.

Getting stakeholders to buy into the new system

For an e-learning project to be successful, change management planning should begin during the project's earliest stages. Gaining buy-in from users is vital. However, because people become comfortable with the status quo, users often find ways to resist or sabotage change, particularly if they feel uninvolved.

When confronted by the possibility of a new or larger e-learning system, the first thing most people want to know is "What's in it for me?" By soliciting

Table 8.1 Assessment of triple constraints

Constraint	Assessment Questions
Scope	• Will the change increase the scope of the project? • Will this increase result in an increase in resources or time? • In order to keep time and resources within their estimates, will the increase in scope result in a decrease in quality?
Time	• Will the change delay the project? • Will the change help to save time and therefore speed up delivery?
Resources	• Will the change consume additional resource? • Will the change produce resource savings?
Quality	• Will the change improve the quality of a deliverable or outcome? • Will the change reduce the quality of a deliverable or outcome?

their concerns up front, addressing them in your plans, and then implementing incremental changes whenever the schedule permits, you'll be most effective. Although such a deliberate approach may take more time, in the end it will help you win internal advocates, instead of enemies.

Case study

Let's look at an example of one change management instance that was delayed more than a year because of a lack of planning. A large university decided to switch from a vendor-based learning management system to an open-source system. The project team's evaluation of both systems indicated they were roughly equivalent in features and functionality. The change management plan incorporated training faculty and students in the new "look and feel" of the system, building on their knowledge and use of the previous vendor product. The team marketed the new system, believed they had built a good case for its use, and asked for volunteers to be in the Fall pilot.

The volunteers surpassed the project team's expectation. The system rolled out in the Fall of 2005 with 50 courses and approximately 5,000 students, approximately 10 percent of their normal e-learning load in the vendor solution. For the first three weeks of the term, all seemed wonderful. The team received rave reviews on the ease of use of the product, how quickly even faculties and students who didn't receive training were able to adapt, and the executive sponsor was complimentary of the introduction. Then the middle of the term arrived with mid-term exams and heightened use and things began to fall apart.

First, the subsystem that handled testing was not as robust as the faculty wished. Why wasn't this identified earlier? Because in initial testing no one actually put the tool through the range of uses it would experience. In fact, the same faculty who loved the system at the beginning of the term – now that they were stressing the testing tool – were complaining loudly that this solution was unacceptable.

Second, after a recommended maintenance patch was applied without thorough testing (due to time constraints), the discussion tool dropped all postings beyond a certain limit. This was without warning. The work around was for the student to modify the post and add the additional information – certainly not a user-friendly solution.

By the end of the 10-week term, 6 of the 50 faculties using the new system were so upset by their experience that they quickly spread the news that the new open-source system was unreliable, difficult to use, and the university had made a big mistake in selecting it. Though the other 42 faculty members also had difficult experiences, they indicated a reluctant but definite willingness to give it a try again if things were changed. Unfortunately, the 6 faculty members who were very upset were strong voices on other committees and that voice spread far and wide outside the pilot of 50 courses to the other 1200+ faculty using the vendor-based system. Soon, there was a call in the faculty senate to stay with the vendor-based system no matter the cost.

The executive sponsor distanced himself from the project, stating "It doesn't matter to me which way we go, as long as faculty are happy." The vision that had initiated the project – one of open-source integration, cost savings, and being a vanguard institution for open-source e-learning – now had no sponsor. Furthermore, recruiting for the next term's volunteers was next to impossible. Any new faculty were reluctant to give it a try – even with promises that the system had improved. Of the 42 from the Fall term who said they would try it again, only 14 ultimately agreed. The rest backed out saying, "As it seems the executive is no longer behind the decision, we don't want to expend the time and energy necessary to make this change."

In a matter of only six weeks, the hard-earned goodwill and accolades for the change had been completely destroyed by the difficult experience of six faculty members, ultimately delaying the project for at least a year and placing it in jeopardy of complete failure. So where did the change management plan fail?

1   Did not plan for testing and implementation during the term in the face of software problems.
2   Did not plan for addressing negative user reactions to how the system worked or didn't work. In fact the optimistic project team did not believe there would be any negative user reaction because they had thoroughly tested the product prior to putting it into production.
3   Did not manage the executive response or plan for how to manage the change if the executive withdrew support.
4   Did not plan for how to move forward (or when not to move forward) in the face of negative impacts.

Characteristics of transformation and change

Whether scaling up an existing e-learning program, or planning to implement an e-learning environment for the first time, these types of change events can be considered major transformations if they impact more than 20 percent of your faculty and staff. In major transformations of large enterprises, executives conventionally focus their attention on devising the best strategic and tactical plans. Thus, project managers tend to focus on that as well. However, to succeed, your change management plan also must have an intimate understanding of the human side of change management – the alignment of the institution's culture, values, people, and behaviors. Plans themselves do not capture value; value is realized only through the sustained, collective actions of the hundreds or thousands of employees who are responsible for designing, executing, and living with the changed environment.

Long-term structural transformation has four characteristics:

1   *Scale* – the change affects all or most of the organization.
2   *Magnitude* – it involves significant alterations of the status quo.
3   *Duration* – it lasts for months, if not years.
4   *Strategic importance* – the organization's ability to deliver e-learning will enhance funding, resources, reputation, and/or student experience.

In all of these characteristics, institutions will reap the rewards only when change occurs at the level of the individual employee. When asked what keeps them up at night, executives involved in transformation often say they are concerned about how the workforce will react, how they can get their team to work together, and how they will be able to lead their organization. They also worry about retaining their organization's unique values and sense of identity, and about creating a culture of commitment and performance. Leadership teams that fail to plan for the human side of change often find themselves wondering why their best-laid plans have gone awry.

10 guiding principles for change management

Most leaders contemplating change know that people matter. It is all too tempting, however, to dwell on the plans and processes of change management rather than face up to the more difficult and more critical human issues. The human side includes people who question the change, sometimes loudly, and respond emotionally. Many managers prefer not to face the human side of change. But incorporating the human side is the key to a good change management plan, and not doing so is almost a sure predictor of project failure. Below are 10 guiding principles for managing change, first articulated in 2004 by John Jones, DeAnne Aguirre, and Matthew Calderone, consulting principals in Booz, Allen, and Hamilton.

1   *Address the "human side" systematically.* Any significant transformation creates "people issues." New leaders will be asked to step up, jobs will be changed, new skills and capabilities must be developed, and employees will be uncertain and resistant. Dealing with these issues on a reactive, case-by-case basis puts speed, morale, and results at risk. A formal approach for managing change – beginning with the leadership team and then engaging key stakeholders and leaders – should be developed early, and adapted often as change moves through the organization. This demands as much data collection and analysis, planning, and implementation discipline as does a redesign of strategy, systems, or processes. The change-management approach should be fully integrated into program design and decision-making, both informing and enabling strategic direction. It should be based on a realistic assessment of the organization's history, readiness, and capacity to change.

2 *Start at the top.* Because change is inherently unsettling for people at all levels of an organization, when it is on the horizon, all eyes will turn to the executive and his or her leadership team for strength, support, and direction. The leaders themselves must embrace the new approaches first, both to challenge and to motivate the rest of the institution. They must speak with one voice and model the desired behaviors. The executive team also needs to understand that, although its public face may be one of unity, it, too, is composed of individuals who are going through stressful times and need to be supported.

3 *Involve every layer.* As transformation programs progress from defining strategy and setting targets to design and implementation, they affect different levels of the organization. Change efforts must include plans for identifying leaders throughout the company and pushing responsibility for design and implementation down, so that change cascades through the organization. At each layer of the organization, the leaders who are identified and trained must be aligned to the company's vision, equipped to execute their specific mission, and motivated to make change happen.

4 *Make the formal case.* Individuals are inherently rational and will question to what extent change is needed, whether the company is headed in the right direction, and whether they want to commit personally to making change happen. They will look to the leadership for answers. The articulation of a formal case for change and the creation of a written vision statement are invaluable opportunities to create or compel leadership–team alignment.

   Three steps should be followed in developing the case:

   i   Articulate a convincing need for change.
   ii   Demonstrate faith that the institution has a future that is inextricably linked to the change, and the leadership is providing the vision to get there.
   iii Provide a road map to guide behavior and decision-making.

   Leaders must then customize this message for various internal audiences, describing the pending change in terms that matter to the individuals.

5 *Create ownership.* Leaders of large change programs must over-perform during the transformation and be the zealots who create a critical mass among the work force in favor of change. This requires more than mere buy-in or passive agreement that the direction of change is acceptable. It demands ownership by leaders willing to accept responsibility for making change happen in all of the areas they influence or control. Ownership is often best created by involving people in identifying problems and crafting solutions. It is reinforced by incentives and rewards. These can be tangible (for example, financial compensation) or psychological (for example, camaraderie and a sense of shared destiny).

6 *Communicate the message.* Too often, change leaders make the mistake of believing that others understand the issues, feel the need to change, and see the new direction as clearly as they do. The best change programs reinforce core messages through regular, timely advice that is both inspirational and practicable. Communications flow in from the bottom and out from the top, and are targeted to provide employees the right information at the right time and to solicit their input and feedback. Often this will require over-communication through multiple, redundant channels.

7 *Assess the cultural landscape.* Successful change programs pick up speed and intensity as they cascade down, making it critically important that leaders understand and account for culture and behaviors at each level of the organization. Companies often make the mistake of assessing culture either too late or not at all. Thorough cultural diagnostics can assess organizational readiness to change, bring major problems to the surface, identify conflicts, and define factors that can recognize and influence sources of leadership and resistance. These diagnostics identify the core values, beliefs, behaviors, and perceptions that must be taken into account for successful change to occur. They serve as the common baseline for designing essential change elements, such as the incorporation of the change into the organizational vision, and building the infrastructure and programs needed to drive change.

8 *Address culture explicitly.* Organizational culture is an amalgam of shared history, explicit values and beliefs, and common attitudes and behaviors. Change programs can involve creating a culture, combining cultures, or reinforcing cultures. Understanding the organization's personal identification is often an effective way to jump-start culture change. For example, if your institution's culture is one of helping the underserved then your change management plan must address how the change will help serve that mission even more effectively. On the other hand, if the culture is to educate the elite minds of your country or the world, then you must address how that will be further enhanced with your project.

9 *Prepare for the unexpected.* No change program goes completely according to plan. People react in unexpected ways; areas of anticipated resistance fall away, while other areas arise; and the external environment shifts. Effectively managing change requires *continual* reassessment of its impact and the organization's willingness and ability to adopt the next wave of transformation. Fed by real data from the field and supported by information and solid decision-making processes, change leaders can then make the adjustments necessary to maintain momentum and drive results.

10 *Speak to the individual.* Change is both an institutional journey and a very personal one. People spend many hours each week at work; many think of their colleagues as a second family. Individuals need to know how their work

will change, what is expected of them during and after the change program, how they will be measured, and what success or failure will mean for them and those around them. Team leaders should be as honest and explicit as possible. People will react to what they see and hear around them, and need to be involved in the change process. Highly visible rewards, such as promotion and recognition will provide dramatic reinforcement for embracing change. Sanction or removal of people standing in the way of change will reinforce the institution's commitment.

Developing and documenting a formal change management plan

The key to your change management plan is to understand and document the people impacted by the change, both in terms of the legitimate needs they have regarding the change and also the personal concerns and potential responses. These are represented as your stakeholders. Stakeholders are people who have some form of interest in the change, whether they are the targets of the change, managers, or other interested parties.

In your initiation phase you identified the stakeholders. In your change management plan you need to identify how they might behave. A lack of stakeholder management is one of the key reasons why change projects fail, so understanding them and ensuring they are addressed in all plans and activities is a critical activity. Your plan should identify differentiated treatment of stakeholders based on their interests, what they really want, any predisposal to be an enemy or an ally, and what power they have over the project.

Mapping stakeholders

Mapping of stakeholders in change can be a useful tool to understand the support and opposition you may face and need to address in your change management plan. You build the map by analyzing your stakeholders and then plotting them, as in Table 8.2, writing their names in the relevant box. A way of

Table 8.2 Stakeholder map

	Opposition		Fence-sitters	Support	
	Active Opponents	Passive Opponents		Passive Supporters	Active Supporters
	High				
Stakeholder Power	**Medium**				
	Low				

doing this in a team is to brainstorm the names of each stakeholder, writing it down on Post-It Notes and sticking them up on a big chart on the wall.

Stakeholder power

Stakeholders all have power, whether it is the formal power invested in a position of authority (in the case of the sponsor or executive) or the social power of being able to persuade others to support or oppose the change. Those with higher power are likely to be your most useful supporters or most dangerous opponents – thus power analysis helps you prioritize your focus on stakeholders.

Active and passive support and resistance

Some people will actively support the change, putting their necks on the line and working long hours to help it succeed. Others will work the other way, vociferously seeking to halt your efforts. These active people are where much focus often happens. However, there is often a silent majority who are more difficult to classify. These may be in gatekeeper positions, where rather than taking positive action, they can subtly support or oppose the change by allowing things to happen or quietly blocking and hindering progress.

Fence-sitters

In the middle are the fence-sitters, who neither support nor oppose the change. They are often playing a waiting game, looking out for who is going to win the game. Once they have made this decision, then they will act. Other fence-sitters are simply undecided. Some people decide quickly while others need more reflection or persuasion. Either way, one of the most important things about fence-sitters is their numbers, which can be significant. Work hard to convert them and you may well win the game.

Accounting for the impact of announced change

How will your stakeholders react when they are told? When change is announced, the results can be significant, which means you should seek to manage the cognitive and behavioral changes from the very beginning. We can guarantee that all stakeholders will not react the same. Some will embrace change and want to move forward quickly, while others will resist change and actually enter into grieving for the "old way" of doing things.

Those who responded negatively to change usually have an initial response of feeling threatened, frightened, or truly have a great deal of philosophical investment in doing things the "traditional" way. One way to document this in your change management plan is by recognizing the Kubler-Ross grief cycle (Table 8.3) and determining how you will address each stage from those

Table 8.3 The Kubler-Ross grief cycle

Stage in Cycle	Emotional Behavior
Shock	Initial paralysis at hearing the bad news.
Denial	Trying to avoid the inevitable.
Anger	Frustrated outpouring of bottled-up emotion.
Bargaining	Seeking for a way out. This is often manifested in touting any other e-learning system but the one you are implementing.
Depression	Realization of the inevitable.
Testing	Seeking realistic solutions. Begins to dabble in participation.
Acceptance	Finally finds the way forward.

stakeholders who react negatively. Also remember that it is important to maintain flexibility in this change management plan throughout the project, as the stages are not linear and some are expressed even after the project is formally completed.

Not all people experience change negatively: some will benefit from the change, while others are people who always find change in itself intriguing and exciting. Though a positive response is a happier reaction for the project team, it can create its own problems which need to be documented in the change management plan. Figure 8.1 diagrams the typical change cycle in an individual with a positive reaction to the change. Note that there is a time when their happy mood changes. To alleviate the length and power of this downward trend, it is important to manage the reactions as much as possible from the beginning.

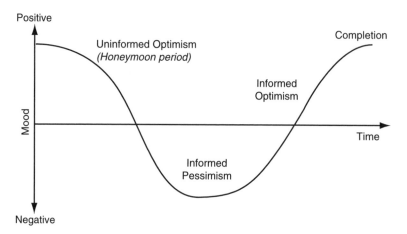

Figure 8.1 Positive change reaction cycle.

Uninformed optimism

In the first stage of positive change, the person is excited and intrigued by the change. They look forward to it with eager anticipation, building a very positive and often over-optimistic view, for example that it will be much easier for them and will resolve all of their current issues. For a time after the change (sometimes sadly short), there is a "honeymoon period," during which they are almost giddy with the change.

Informed pessimism

The honeymoon period does not last forever and the rose-tinted glasses start to fade as the untidiness of reality starts to bite. The person finds that things have not all fallen into place, that other people have not magically become as cooperative as they expected, and that things are just not as easy as they had anticipated. This pushes them into a period of gloom when they realize that perfection is not that easy to attain. This may evidence itself in mutterings and grumblings. If managed effectively, this stage does not reach the depths of the depression stage mentioned above in Kubler-Ross's grief cycle. However, if managed ineffectively the person drops into a delayed negative cycle.

Informed optimism

Before long, however, their original optimism starts to reassert itself, now tinted by a resignation to the reality of the situation. After all, things are not that bad, and a positive sense of potential begins to creep back. As they look around them and talk to other people, they make realistic plans and move forward with an informed sense of optimism.

Completion

Eventually, things reach a relatively steady platform of realistic and workable action. The person is probably happier than they were before the change started and, with their realistic vision, have the potential to reach even better heights of happiness as they achieve more of their potential.

The key in making the initial announcement is to avoid a mess of miscommunication, innuendo, and active sabotage, which results in a change environment that resembles open warfare. Instead you must manage the initial announcement. Rather than just announce a change, first think about the effects that it will have and stage the communication in a way to have the impact and effect that you desire.

Resistance

No matter how well you manage the announcement or the process, there will be resistance. You need to identify how your stakeholders might push back against the change. Resistance to change is the action taken by individuals and groups when they perceive that a change that is occurring as a threat to them. Key words here are "perceive" and "threat." The threat need not be real or large for resistance to occur.

Resistance may take many forms, including active or passive, overt or covert, individual or organized, aggressive or timid. The key is determining how you are going to manage resistance; what processes will be put into place to spot resistance early and deal with it.

Breaking down the change management task

One of the key problems in change is managing the balance between people responses and just getting things done. Though the people side is often not taken into consideration nearly enough, it is also possible to spend too much time dealing with people and forget the nitty-gritty detail of getting things done to complete the project.

The scope of the change is the largest determiner of impact, and thus the approach that is needed to manage it. The scope includes both "what" and "who" affect the size of the project. A small change can be done on the fly, while changing multiple systems or cultures is not so easy. The following seven items should minimally be addressed in your plan:

1   *What is changed* – One dimension of scope is the amount of things that are changed.
2   *Scope of impact* – When some things are changed, they have a significant ripple on other things. Thus, for example, changing a company policy or an organizational goal will have a very broad impact on whoever is involved.
3   *Amount of work* – The "what" of change equates to the amount of work that needs to be done. This does not necessarily equate to how many people are affected, for example where the change work involves few people, but stretches over a long period of time.
4   *Complexity of work* – Some work is easy to do, while other work requires significant expertise, such as when new course products or a complex learning management system needs to be developed or integrated. Complex work needs expert people who are expensive and who do not always agree with you. Complex work also brings with it risks of failure that need to be managed.
5   *Who is changed* – As discussed above, the most difficult work of change is often around people.

6   *Numbers of people* – When you have to change a lot of people then, even if the change is small, the job will not be that easy. When you have a lot of people to change, then you increase the chances of resistance.

7   *Degree of resistance* – If you are going to implement a change that will be highly unpopular into an organization where authority is devolved to a low level (for example where most people are "professionals"), then you must expect a significant level of resistance.

Four levels of scope

Combining the above "what" and "who", four common scopes of change can be identified, in Table 8.4, in which different approaches may be used.

Change complexity analysis

Change complexity analysis seeks to identify how difficult a change project will be. The more complex the project, the more carefully the project will need to be managed. Complexity may be plotted along two axes: task complexity and people complexity. The resultant position may lead to very different approaches to managing the change.

Task complexity

Start by identifying the complexity of the task involved in the change *without* considering the people issues. Some of the factors which affect task complexity are indicated in Table 8.5.

People complexity

The major additional complexity that change projects add over other projects is the potential problems around people. It is thus important to consider the people complexity separately from the task complexity. Some of the factors which affect people complexity are indicated in Table 8.6.

Table 8.4 Four levels of scope and change processes

	Small What	Big What
Small who	**Fine tuning** Do it on the fly.	**Standard project** Separate project manager. No special change methods.
Big who	**Local transformation** Engage everyone involved in the change.	**Major transformation** Use change teams. Engage all major players. Lots of human change.

Table 8.5 Task complexity analysis

Factor	Description
Number of tasks	The more things there are to do, the more complex managing the whole show is.
Variety of tasks	If there are lots of similar tasks then similar tools, management methods, etc., may be used.
Complexity of tasks	More difficult tasks require greater attention and have more ways to fail. It also makes it more difficult to verify.
Verifiability of work	If you can't see what has been done then it is difficult to track progress and check that things are done right.
Number of locations	Doing the job in many different places makes coordination more difficult and requires more travel.
Interdependencies between tasks	When one change depends on others or can affect many things, it is more complex than when changes are independent of one another.
Time pressures	When time is limited, there is no time to correct errors.
Financial constraints	When money is tight, you may be limited in such as the quality of what is used.
Quality criteria	When quality requirements are high, then there are more ways to get it wrong.

Build the change management plan

When planning for change, you need to consider both the actions to make the change and the problems you might meet in gaining the required commitment to carry the actions through. You do this by matching "styles of change" to the scope. Depending on the style and scope/size of the change, different approaches are likely to be taken. This is often a matter of management preference and situational factors. Let's look at four styles of change that are typically used in organizations: collaborative, consultative, directive, and coercive.

Collaborative

A collaborative approach to change means involving the people affected, creating the change *with* them rather than doing the change *to* them. This works by gaining commitment through getting people to invest in the change.

A big dilemma with collaboration is the extent to which you allow people to make decisions versus make recommendations about the change. Risks with giving away too much power include people making sub-optimal, self-oriented choices or the devolved decisions across the organization not aligning with one another and hence creating more problems than they solve.

Table 8.6 People complexity analysis

Factor	Description
People numbers	More people means more communication – and geometrically so as potential conversations rise with the square of the numbers of people.
Diversity	Different people means different languages, different cultures, different "political correctness," etc.
Emotional intelligence	When people are emotionally not ready for the change, then the shock of the change will make them dysfunctional for longer.
Social cohesion	When people are split into many different social groups then each group may well require a different approach.
Political style	If the prevailing political style is divisive and devious then change will be far more difficult.
Power balance	If the balance of power must change then those that hold power are likely to fight to hold onto it.
Sponsor commitment	If those who are legitimizing the change do not give their full and visible support, then people affected by the change will also be less committed.
Learning requirement	When you are doing something new, it is more difficult if you are repeating a change you have done before.
Uncertainty	If the change plans are uncertain and unstable then there is likely be more discomfort as well as more arguments.
Personal change	If people must change beliefs, values, etc. (such as in culture change) then this is more difficult than a simple change of activities.
Change skills	If the people managing the change have not done this before then they may lack the ability to do it effectively.

A way of making collaboration successful is the ***what-how*** approach. In this method, the senior team leaders still control the strategic decisions and work out ***what*** needs doing. They then devolve ***how*** this is to be achieved to the organization below them, in which more what-how deployments may occur.

Collaborative approaches are particularly important when you have a high level of professionally qualified people whose brains may be usefully engaged in the planning process and who would be particularly dismayed at being left out. This is why academic institutions are known for collaborative decision-making. The collaborative approach becomes even more important if you are in an employment market where your people can easily leave to work in other companies.

Collaboration also may be the only approach when power is distributed across the company and you simply are unable to implement change without the full buy-in of large groups of people.

Collaborative approaches can require significant amounts of time and effort, and so may be restricted to situations where you have the foresight to change before it is thrust upon you. The problem with collaboration is that it takes time and effort, which relatively few organizations are either willing or able to give. When speed is important and resources are thin on the ground, then investing in collaborative efforts can seem wasteful.

Consultative

A compromise to the full-on collaborative approach is to show that at least you are listening to the people affected by the change. This may take the form of interactive real-time "town hall" meetings, directors' tours, and so on. It can use technology for Web-enabled discussions and so on. It may also use suggestion boxes or comment boxes. Consultation is, in many ways, a watered-down version of collaboration. The views of people are elicited, which does take some time, but any protracted period of debate is eliminated. This sometimes allows for an acceptable decision without having to get a lot to be part of the decision-making process.

Care must be taken during consultation to ensure that people know the process, and that they perceive it to be fair. As you move away from collaboration, greater trust is required of the decision-makers and thus more trust-building activities may be required on the front-end of the process.

Consultative approaches provide a degree of balance between the engagement of collaboration and the push of direction or coercion. When collaboration is deemed too time-consuming, the consultative approach still enhances stakeholder buy-in.

Directive

In a directive approach, there may still be a high level of communication, but it is now largely one-way. The organization is *told* how it will change. With the control of what happens in relatively few hands, the risk of variation in the plan is essentially removed.

What will happen and when is laid out in a schedule that may or may not be publicized. The problem with this is that there is often a fear (which may or may not be well-founded) that there will be greater resistance to change if people know what is going to happen. Resistance comes particularly from those who hold power. Remember, even the most junior person can have a great deal of influence and power.

To help reduce the problem of resistance, very high levels of communication may be required and the leadership making the decisions need to be seen in a beneficent paternal or maternal role – father knows best and has not failed you before, or mother cares only for your well-being. If the culture is one where this type of leadership has been in place and accepted, the directive approach will not pose a problem. However, if the culture is one of collaboration or consultation, then the directive approach will be absolutely rejected.

Directive approaches require the leadership to have the power to make this work, particularly getting people to move in the same direction rather than scattering as they run away from the push of change. Thus, direction needs to be done firmly and quickly. This approach suits situations where time is of the essence. Strong planning is essential to make it work, as you seldom have time to go back and try something else. You also are leaving out the thoughts of a lot of other minds so you need to take time to get it right first time.

Coercive

At the furthest extreme, a coercive approach pays little attention to the people, their ideas, or their needs. Changes are implemented in a relatively mechanical way, and the leadership presents it as a "like it or leave" approach – placing immediate threat of job security on those who may consider resisting.

Not all coercive approaches are unethical and some are simply born of the need for urgency. Ethics lie in the values of the people who are planning and implementing the change, rather than the fact that a coercive approach is being used.

Even more so than direction, coercive approaches suit only those situations where you need people to move particularly fast or where human relations have broken down to the point where nobody listens to anyone else and the only option is force. Of course this is not a desirable option, but when the alternative is total failure, it may be the best (or only) choice of action.

The change delivery plan

The change delivery plan lays out the path whereby the change will be implemented. This is often a difficult and hazardous journey and needs to include a strong commitment plan to ensure the right people are fully engaged and properly motivated.

An aligned organization has no waste, as everything fits cleanly with everything else. A misaligned organization has people working at cross-purposes, with conflict as a common feature. In an aligned organization, people agree and work smoothly together to an effective purpose. Doing change in the right order is important to making it successful. Creating alignment thus starts with drivers, then moves to processes, then technology, organization, and people.

The commitment plan

Many effective change management plans have a significant focus on communication. This is a very important part of most change efforts, yet it is not the real intent, which is perhaps why many change efforts do not take it seriously. Communication can easily seem to be a lot of effort for little return.

What is *really* being sought in communication is that people become *committed* to the change, collaborating with the work rather than resisting it or complying unwillingly. The commitment plan should thus be focused on what will cause people to become *and* remain committed to the change. It is one thing to get them excited with a visionary start or an internal marketing strategy. It is another to keep them with you when issues are appearing everywhere and there is still no sight of the promised land.

Stakeholder understanding

To build commitment requires a start point of understanding the stakeholders' questions, both in terms of what drives them and how they may respond to change. As discussed early in this chapter, mapping stakeholders helps to begin this process and reinforces the need to plan for different treatments for different stakeholders' interests and needs.

Predictable change

One of the key needs that a change management plan tries to address is the ability to predict what will happen, and thus gain a sense of control. A way of building more commitment is to show that the change is an unstoppable train. Whenever something is promised, it always happens. This means being careful with promises, of course, and perhaps conservative with plans. It is far more effective in building trust and commitment to complete actions ahead of plan rather than behind plan.

The plan thus becomes the predictable island of stability in the sea of change. When people are uncertain of everything else, at least the plan is predictable.

Evidence of change

Change and commitment includes a great deal about trust, and long-term trust is founded on evidence. To create a real acceptance of the change, there are two common ways of building commitment. First is the impact method, where large amounts of change are bundled together to show *how much* has changed. Second is the dripping-tap method, where a steady stream of evidence is used to keep the change up-front and visible.

The impact method is often used early on, with a big marketing kickoff. The problem with this is that it sets excessive expectations which, when they are not delivered, result in cynicism and a nose-dive in commitment. The impact method is most effective on small projects that will be completed in under six months and have immediate evidence of positive result.

The dripping-tap method starts more slowly, but has a more certain progress, with regular news from the front of changes that have happened and planned actions taken on track. It works through gradually building commitment with clear evidence rather than trying to grab it all at once. This plays more to how most people give commitment, not freely and instantly, but carefully and only after there is clear and repeated evidence. This method requires a lot more planning and management, and is best used for large projects which require many months or years to complete.

Executive sponsorship and change management traps

Few change management plans prepare for a change in vision, scope, or objectives. Unfortunately, this happens more frequently than most project managers realize. These types of changes cause the project manager to return to the initiation and planning phases of project management and rework initial specifications and deliverables lists. These new specifications then ripple forward throughout all other planning and documentation and can be quite frustrating. This level of change is one of the key challenges of project management, and it does happen with surprising frequency. Most often the reason it happens is that the sponsor was not managed.

Mismanaging sponsorship is perhaps one of the main reasons why change projects fail. A common sponsorship trap occurs where sponsors see their role as an early agreement, but with no further engagement plus an open option to back out at any time. Such weak commitment is highly hazardous and must be exposed and managed if the change is to succeed.

Another trap for the project manager is not engaging sponsors early on, either through not realizing they exist or by assuming they will be no problem. When the project gets under way and things start to change, these people then feel left out and may become obstructionists.

When things are going wrong, if your sponsors are washing their hands of the project, then you are doomed. Managed well, however, they will find it impossible to wash their hands because you have ensured that they are involved in the decision-making process. Good management also ensures they are well-connected into the project, not only physically but also mentally and emotionally.

Chief executive officers (CEOs) and senior business leaders are not all created equal. Some will naturally lead change and be effective sponsors. If this is your executive, then you are in good hands and it is likely that major changes in scope, goals, or objectives will not occur. However, in other organizations executives may express the desire to sponsor the change, but lack the knowledge and skills to do it effectively. These executives need direct support and coaching to be effective sponsors of change. This can still be a good situation for the project team, but it places the onus squarely on the project manager to assist the executive in sponsoring the change.

Unfortunately, yet other executives do not fall into either of the above types. Whether through a lack of knowledge about change management, or a personal management style, these executives usually fall into one of three categories:

1   *The delegator* – The executive is uncomfortable performing the activities necessary to sponsor the change and would rather delegate these duties to someone else. This can work to your advantage if the person who has been delegated the task is an enthusiastic supporter of the change and has the executive's full backing. However, often the tasks are delegated to someone who is equally uncomfortable with change management and it is delegated yet again. With each delegation, the executive sponsorship is watered down – leaving your team with no real executive sponsorship. This then changes the way you manage the entire project and introduces a large risk factor that scope, goals, and objectives are likely to change in the midst of the project plan.

2   *The distancer* – The executive does not believe that their involvement is necessary for the change to be a success and do not see why their involvement is important. This executive is similar to the delegator in that the responsibility is placed lower on the hierarchy of managers. However, because the executive does not believe their involvement is necessary at all, you really have no buy-in at the top level and have to negotiate all decisions with much larger constituencies to ensure that the project moves forward with clear goals and objectives. It also means that the chance of complications and change in scope, goals, and objectives is that much more likely.

3   *The seesawer* – This executive is an enthusiastic sponsor as long as the project is popular. However, from the moment they hear the first complaint, they quickly distance themselves from the project and any decision-making surrounding it. The seesaw may begin as early as the first person raising issues about the project (even if it is one person out of a thousand) or as late as when more drastic measures occur. The key is that whenever the seesaw direction changes, your project is in jeopardy. Some project managers are lured into a false confidence when the seesaw changes up and down, believing that the ups will win. If you wait until the project has many naysayers, you can be guaranteed that this type of executive will stop the project cold.

A part of your risk assessment and change management plan must take into account the type of executive sponsor(s) (or lack of sponsorship) the project has. This is not the time to look at your work environment through rose-colored glasses. This is the time to carefully evaluate the politics in your organization and make sure that your change management plan includes the worst-case scenario. You may never need to use it, but if it does happen you will be prepared and you will still have a chance of saving the project.

The challenge for many project teams is what to do with senior executives and presidents or CEOs who fall into one of the three above categories. The project manager and the change management team must do something to improve sponsorship in these types of scenario.

One approach is not to have large projects rely on only one or two executive sponsors. Instead, have many executives involved. This makes it more difficult for a single person to control the success or failure of the project, and when your relationship with one executive may be going downhill another one may be able to intervene on your behalf and help to keep the project on track.

As project manager, you need to have a good understanding of the nature of sponsorship and carefully assist and manage the various sponsors in the project. In project management circles there is often discussion of four different types of sponsors that you need to manage: initiating sponsor, key sponsor, primary sponsors, and secondary sponsors.

1   *Initiating sponsor* – This is the person who starts the change project and may well be the person with whom you meet at the first meeting. This person may be the key sponsor or may be someone lower in the organization. He or she may well be the person who asks you to manage or facilitate the change project.

2   *Key sponsor* – This is the *one* person (often the most senior manager) who can resolve the stickiest of problems, such as differences between other primary sponsors, and who provides the ultimate authority for the project, and may have a hand in direction and approval. You will need to spend quality time up-front with the key sponsor to understand his or her real needs. You should then meet regularly enough to ensure that he or she is in the loop and remains committed. If the key sponsor drifts away and shows insufficient interest, then you may have to consider closing down the project.

3   *Primary sponsors* – This is a small group of managers whose support is critical and who have sufficient clout to unblock most problems, including problems with secondary sponsors. They are sometimes also called "sustaining sponsors" and often work together as a core team. To get the time and commitment of the primary sponsors that you need, you will need to spend time with them, both individually and collectively, showing how close collaboration is very much in their interests (if it is not, then you need to connect with the key sponsor over this). You will also need to put appropriate effort into building this group into a cohesive and effective team.

4   *Secondary sponsors* – These are managers whose support is needed, albeit

at a limited level. They are important as they have the ability to block change. However, if they were all to be members of the core team, then that team would become unwieldy and difficult to manage. Excluding them from this team, however, can be a bad political move as they then may take revenge by refusing to cooperate or otherwise block progress. They require careful handling and usually need to be communicated with on a regular basis. If you can't invite them to all meetings, then at least you can keep them up to date with progress and show how you are listening to them and taking their concerns into account.

The role of sponsors

The sponsors of the project can play a number of roles in the change project. The only role that they must not be allowed to play is sitting back and letting you get on with it. If any of these roles is not undertaken, then it will be necessary to discuss how it will be effectively performed. For example, the gatekeeper role may be played by an assigned manager. It is important that these roles are clearly blessed by the appropriate sponsor, and that sponsors will provide clear leadership, plus consistent and final arbitration in any disputes. Table 8.7 illustrates some of the roles that are critical to your change management plan.

All of these are key roles in your change management plan, and a plan to communicate regularly with these sponsors and make sure they are committed to the project should be included at every predicted change step.

Table 8.7 Roles critical to the change management plan

Role	Actions
Visionary	Presenting and selling his or her vision of the new future, motivating people to work towards this future.
Gatekeeper	Reviewing progress at defined milestones or "gates," and only allowing continuation if milestone criteria are met.
Moneybags	Holding the budget for changes and only paying for those projects and changes which meet the change criteria.
Unblocker	Acting to remove resistance and other organizational blocks that hinder the changes being implemented.
Mediator	Resolving disputes between people affected by the change.
Planner	Active involvement in planning the change, then reviewing implementation of the change.
Leader	Full involvement in all stages of the change.

Chapter 9

Putting it all together

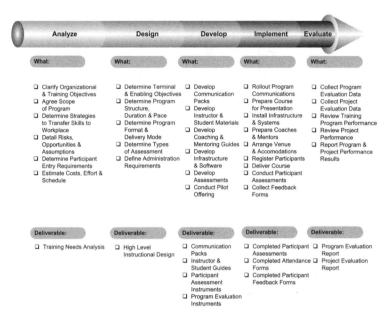

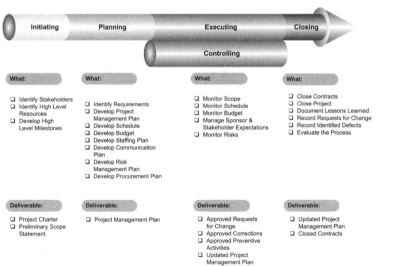

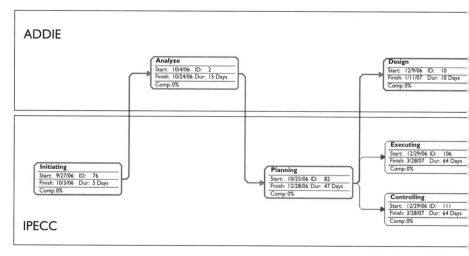

Figure 9.1 Network diagram overview.

In Chapters 2 through 6 we discussed all the stages of ADDIE and the phases of IPECC independently. Though we provided examples of process integration between these two models, the amount of information we covered can be overwhelming. It is possible that you feel like you are in the deep end of the swimming pool, barely keeping your head above water as you try to integrate these two models and all the concepts into one cohesive and quality-based process.

This chapter will help to put it all together with step-by-step pictures and discussion of the entire integrated process and its sequencing. We will do this by looking at the integrated project schedule using a desktop scheduling application, Microsoft Project. We will follow each step of the process and illustrate how the deliverables explicate both the ADDIE and IPECC processes at the same time.

The figure at the top of this chapter illustrates the relationship of the two processes, identifies actions that are performed in each of the respective processes and the corresponding deliverables from those processes. You may wish to make a separate photocopy of this figure, as you will be returning to it frequently. We will refer to this as the "master diagram" as it guides us through the remainder of this chapter.

Network diagram

A network diagram is used to display the logical sequence of activities. Logically, this is a timeline of the project activities – customarily drawn from left to right. Each box on the diagram is used to illustrate an activity (task) or summary task. One might assume that the length of the box depicts the duration of

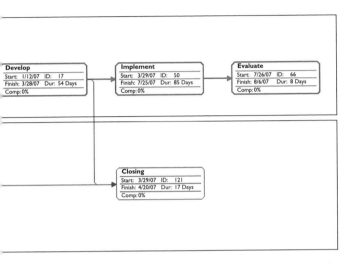

the activity – this is not the case. Each box is the same size irrespective of the duration of the task. Tasks are connected by lines to indicate precedence. In our network diagram for the entire process, we have organized ADDIE stages in the upper half of the graphic and IPECC phases in the lower half of the diagram (see Figure 9.1).

When starting a new schedule, it is typical to develop the WBS first, as we did in Chapter 3. However, to provide an overview of how we believe ADDIE stages and IPECC phases interact, we will introduce the network diagram first, and then move to the WBS for the entire project.

The initiating phase of IPECC is the first phase of the project. In the initiating phase, you will interact with key stakeholders and the sponsor to create the project charter. After you have completed the project charter, you should develop the project management plan with members of your project team. However, in order to develop the project management plan fully, you will need information collected and analyzed in the analyze stage of ADDIE. The network diagram for the project illustrates this relationship (see Figure 9.2).

Upon completion of the planning phase, the executing and controlling phases occur simultaneously with the design and develop stages of ADDIE (see Figure 9.2). Considering the opening illustration in this chapter, this is evident. However, in Figure 9.2, it appears that the executing and controlling phases end with design. Remember that the size of the boxes in a network diagram does not indicate task duration, instead the diagram illustrates task sequence.

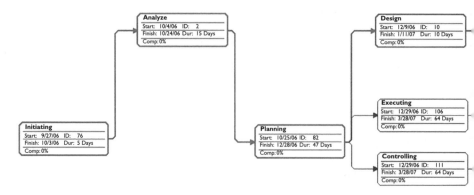

Figure 9.2 Integrated ADDIE–IPECC network diagram.

The integrated ADDIE–IPECC WBS

Now that we have introduced the sequencing of ADDIE stages and IPECC phases, we'd like to discuss the integration of ADDIE and IPECC deliverables for a non-iterated project. The master diagram illustrates *what* we believe should be done in each ADDIE stage and IPECC phase to develop the respective deliverable. Let's look at the first *what* depicted on the master diagram. It is under the "analyze" stage and lists several tasks that need to occur.

- Clarify organizational and training objectives.
- Agree scope of program.
- Determine strategies to transfer skills to workplace.
- Detail risks, opportunities, and assumptions.
- Determine participant entry requirements.
- Estimate costs, effort, and schedule.

In other words, the **what** provides the task outline for all the items needed to develop the specified **deliverable** – the training needs analysis. These two are then easily integrated in the WBS, where the deliverable acts as the summary task and the subtasks are the breakdown structure needed to accomplish development of that deliverable. So, the master diagram actually outlines the integrated ADDIE–IPECC processes for your e-learning project.

To illustrate this process further, Table 9.1 shows the ADDIE stage summary tasks and task IDs along with the IPECC phase summary tasks and task IDs.

Figure 9.3 (Integrated ADDIE–IPECC work breakdown structure) illustrates how the deliverables for each ADDIE stage and IPECC phase are actually placed into a WBS structure. Investigating the left two columns of Figure 9.3 you will find each ADDIE stage and IPECC phase, and the corresponding deliverable, illustrated in the opening figure of this chapter.

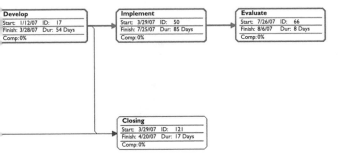

Table 9.1 Task ID associated with ADDIE–
IPECC models

ADDIE Stage/IPECC Phase	Task ID
ADDIE	I
Analyze	2
Design	10
Develop	17
Implement	50
Evaluate	66
IPECC	75
Initiating	76
Planning	82
Executing	106
Controlling	111
Closing	122

The right two columns of Figure 9.3 provide a Gantt chart of the project and the duration of each task or summary task. An example of the time period of a summary task is indicated by the duration marked for task ID 1, the entire ADDIE process, which is 219 days. An example of a shorter time period for a smaller task is Task ID 122, the closed contracts deliverable, which has a duration of 1 day. Durations for summary tasks are computed by adding the respective durations of the individual tasks that create the summary task. Take a look at another example of this in summary task 121, the closing phase. The duration of closing is 17 days, which is the sum of the durations of individual tasks 122 through 127.

Given that you have identified all of the deliverables, how do you now develop them? Let's take each of the ADDIE stages and IPECC phases in the sequence

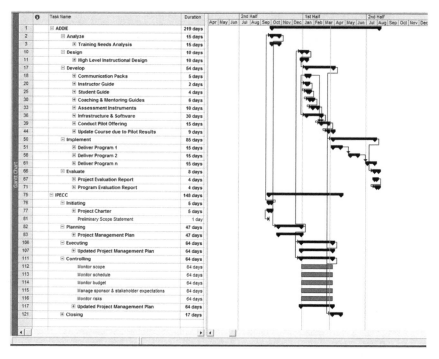

Figure 9.3 Integrated ADDIE–IPECC work breakdown structure.

illustrated in the network diagram (Figure 9.2) and see how this all works together.

Ideally, we would like to provide a single figure for the integrated ADDIE–IPECC stages and phases; however, the figure would cover approximately two pages in this text which might be hard to follow. Instead, we will break the figure into each ADDIE stage or IPECC phase. The sequence of these figures will follow the sequence illustrated in the network diagram (Figure 9.2).

The first stage or process that we execute is IPECC initiating. Figure 9.4 illustrates the outline of the activities to create the deliverables from the initiating phase. Note how items 78–80 indicate exactly what you need to do to develop the deliverable, the project charter.

The analyze stage then follows the completion of initiating. Figure 9.5 illustrates the outline of the activities to create the deliverable from the analyze stage, the training needs analysis.

Again the tasks required to develop the deliverable are clearly delineated as subtasks on the WBS (items 4–9).

Following the completion of the analyze stage, you will develop the project management plan, the deliverable from the planning phase of IPECC (see Figure 9.6). This is the IPECC phase that takes most of the project team's time

ID	ⓘ	Task Name	Duration	1st Half								2nd Half	
				Sep	Oct	Nov	Dec	Jan	Feb	Mar	Apr	May	Jun	Jul	Aug
75		IPECC	148 days										
76		Initiating	5 days										
77		Project Charter	5 days										
78		Identify stakeholders	2 days										
79		Identify high level resources	1 day										
80		Develop high level milestones	2 days										
81		Preliminary Scope Statement	1 day										

Figure 9.4 Outline of activities to develop the project charter and preliminary scope statement.

ID	ⓘ	Task Name	Duration	1st Half								2nd Half	
				Sep	Oct	Nov	Dec	Jan	Feb	Mar	Apr	May	Jun	Jul	Aug
1		ADDIE	219 days										
2		Analyze	15 days										
3		Training Needs Analysis	15 days										
4		Clarify organizational & training objectives	1 day										
5		Agree scope of program	1 day										
6		Determine strategies to transfer skills to workplace	3 days										
7		Detail risks, opportunities & assumptions	2 days										
8		Determine participant entry requirements	10 days										
9		Estimate costs, effort & schedule	5 days										

Figure 9.5 Outline of activities to develop the training needs analysis.

ID	ⓘ	Task Name	Duration	1st Half								2nd Half	
				Sep	Oct	Nov	Dec	Jan	Feb	Mar	Apr	May	Jun	Jul	Aug
75		IPECC	148 days										
76		Initiating	5 days										
82		Planning	47 days										
83		Project Management Plan	47 days										
84		Scope definition	2 days										
85		Work Breakdown Structure	20 days										
86		Risk management plan	3 days										
87		Identify potential risks	1 day										
88		Assess potential risks	1 day										
89		Select risk response	1 day										
90		Change management plan	2 days										
91		Develop request for change form	1 day										
92		Develop change management process	1 day										
93		Schedule	5 days										
94		Develop network diagram	1 day										
95		Determine activity relationships	1 day										
96		Determine resource requirements	1 day										
97		Estimate activity duration	2 days										
98		Budget	3 days										
99		Identify cost of resources	3 days										
100		Staffing plan	4 days										
101		Identify skill requirements	1 day										
102		Identify staff	2 days										
103		Plan staff resource requirements	1 day										
104		Communication management plan	3 days										
105		Procurement plan	5 days										

Figure 9.6 Outline of activities to develop the project management plan.

as this deliverable and its tasks provide all of the important information needed for the rest of the project.

Unlike the previous two examples, note that the project management plan is a summary task and deliverable. It has several subtasks and deliverables associated with it. Consequently, the time periods required to complete each task and deliverable all roll up to total the entire duration required for the project management plan.

The design stage of ADDIE is next, where the executing and controlling phases of IPECC are implemented simultaneously. Figure 9.7 illustrates the outline of the activities to create the deliverable from the ADDIE design stage and the executing and controlling phases of IPECC.

The ADDIE develop stage is also a part of the IPECC executing and controlling phases. Figure 9.8 illustrates the outline of the activities to create the deliverable from the design stage and executing and controlling phases.

As an example of how course modules might be included in the WBS, in Figure 9.8, we have illustrated the development of three modules of a course. They are labeled module 1, module 2, and module n. You will notice the various subtasks associated with module development by investigating task IDs 21 through 23 that develop the instructor notes, and task IDs 26 through 28 that develop the student materials. After the pilot offering of the course, task ID 39, the course may need to be updated. Task IDs 45 through 47 are then the update tasks for both the instructor and student materials. You will want to modify this WBS template to reflect the number of modules you plan to develop for each course. This course structure can then be replicated for however many courses are included in your project.

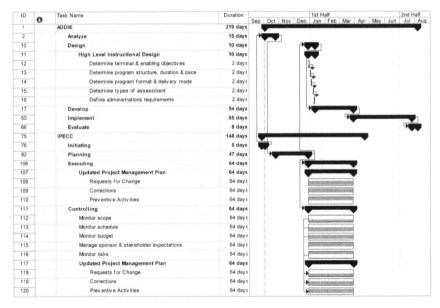

Figure 9.7 Combined activities from the ADDIE design stage and IPECC executing and controlling phases.

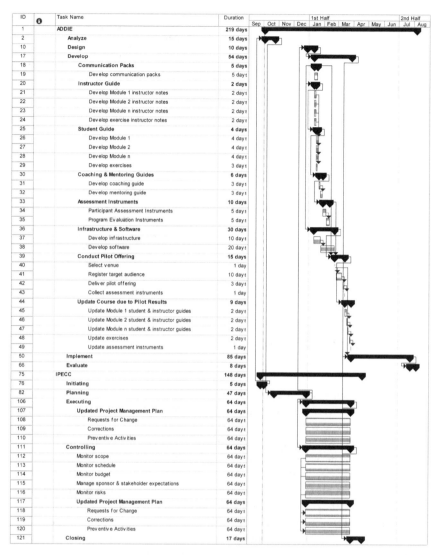

ID	❶	Task Name	Duration	1st Half	2nd Half
1		ADDIE	219 days		
2		Analyze	15 days		
10		Design	10 days		
17		Develop	54 days		
18		Communication Packs	5 days		
19		Develop communication packs	5 days		
20		Instructor Guide	2 days		
21		Develop Module 1 instructor notes	2 days		
22		Develop Module 2 instructor notes	2 days		
23		Develop Module n instructor notes	2 days		
24		Develop exercise instructor notes	2 days		
25		Student Guide	4 days		
26		Develop Module 1	4 days		
27		Develop Module 2	4 days		
28		Develop Module n	4 days		
29		Develop exercises	3 days		
30		Coaching & Mentoring Guides	6 days		
31		Develop coaching guide	3 days		
32		Develop mentoring guide	3 days		
33		Assessment Instruments	10 days		
34		Participant Assessment Instruments	5 days		
35		Program Evaluation Instruments	5 days		
36		Infrastructure & Software	30 days		
37		Develop infrastructure	10 days		
38		Develop software	20 days		
39		Conduct Pilot Offering	15 days		
40		Select venue	1 day		
41		Register target audience	10 days		
42		Deliver pilot offering	3 days		
43		Collect assessment instruments	1 day		
44		Update Course due to Pilot Results	9 days		
45		Update Module 1 student & instructor guides	2 days		
46		Update Module 2 student & instructor guides	2 days		
47		Update Module n student & instructor guides	2 days		
48		Update exercises	2 days		
49		Update assessment instruments	1 day		
50		Implement	85 days		
66		Evaluate	8 days		
75		IPECC	148 days		
76		Initiating	5 days		
82		Planning	47 days		
106		Executing	64 days		
107		Updated Project Management Plan	64 days		
108		Requests for Change	64 days		
109		Corrections	64 days		
110		Preventive Activities	64 days		
111		Controlling	64 days		
112		Monitor scope	64 days		
113		Monitor schedule	64 days		
114		Monitor budget	64 days		
115		Manage sponsor & stakeholder expectations	64 days		
116		Monitor risks	64 days		
117		Updated Project Management Plan	64 days		
118		Requests for Change	64 days		
119		Corrections	64 days		
120		Preventive Activities	64 days		
121		Closing	17 days		

Figure 9.8 Outline of activities from the develop stage and executing and controlling phases.

The final integrated processes are the ADDIE implement stage and the IPECC closing phase. Figure 9.9 illustrates the outline of the activities to create the deliverables from these processes.

In this example, we have completed the project and the course is ready to be delivered. We will now transition the course from our project team to the organization responsible for the operation of the course. In this WBS, we have

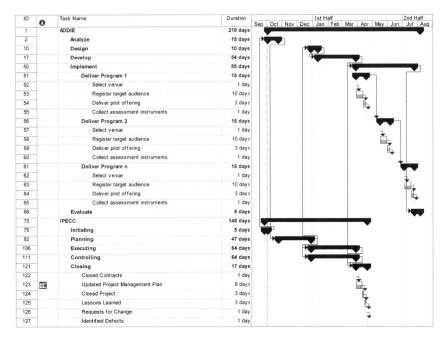

Figure 9.9 Outline of activities to implement and close the project.

illustrated the delivery of the course three times, task IDs 51, 56, and 61. This is for example purposes only; your institution may deliver the course many more times or certainly fewer.

As a part of closing the project, we include the ADDIE evaluate stage. Continuing through the WBS, we need to consider the activities needed to evaluate the course (see Figure 9.10).

Now, you have all the steps illustrated. Remember, this entire project plan, along with all of the templates discussed throughout this book, can be found on the companion website to this text (http://www.routledge.com/textbooks/ 9780415772204). This should give you a good starting point if you choose to use a desktop scheduling program to plan and schedule your project.

How rapid prototyping affects the WBS

Up to this point, we have discussed the WBS to develop a course using a non-iterative ADDIE process. The authors believe that the development of an e-learning course is somewhat similar to the development of a new software application. Many information technology and/or consulting organizations are applying rapid application development processes to develop new software applications.

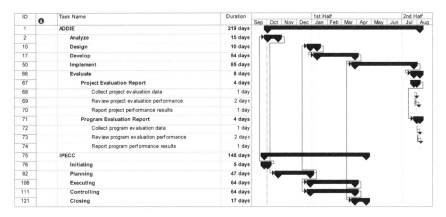

ID	❶	Task Name	Duration	Sep	Oct	Nov	Dec	Jan	Feb	Mar	Apr	May	Jun	Jul	Aug
1		**ADDIE**	219 days												
2		Analyze	15 days												
10		Design	10 days												
17		Develop	54 days												
50		Implement	85 days												
66		Evaluate	8 days												
67		Project Evaluation Report	4 days												
68		Collect project evaluation data	1 day												
69		Review project evaluation performance	2 days												
70		Report project performance results	1 day												
71		Program Evaluation Report	4 days												
72		Collect program evaluation data	1 day												
73		Review program evaluation performance	2 days												
74		Report program performance results	1 day												
75		**IPECC**	148 days												
76		Initiating	5 days												
82		Planning	47 days												
106		Executing	64 days												
111		Controlling	64 days												
121		Closing	17 days												

Figure 9.10 Outline of activities to evaluate the course.

Rapid development processes are founded on the practice of developing a prototype of the software application or one aspect of the application, say the navigation, and testing this aspect through a user acceptance test. This user acceptance test may be convening a small panel from the target audience to view and navigate a prototype of the application using the designed navigation. Collected impressions of the new navigation technique then provide the input to the next phase of the project which might be to change the navigation technique due to analysis of the collected feedback from the target audience or to continue with the development of the new application because the test of the navigation was successful.

We suggest that a similar process might be used in the design and development of an e-learning course. This process may help to cut down on time needed for design, development, and testing. It can also prove particularly advantageous when you are developing multiple related courses, such as in an entire degree program, which may have 20 or 30 course possibilities.

This rapid prototyping process is iterative (see Figure 9.11) instead of linear. In this process the design and development cycle is repeated with each mini-evaluation, which then informs the next design-development cycle, until a prototype is accepted and tested. Then the prototype is replicated – often in the form of templates – throughout the remaining courses.

This concept was introduced in Chapter 5, where we discussed the formative evaluation portion of the process. Figure 9.11 illustrates an example where the development of the course has been subdivided into three prototypes followed by the development of the final course. At the end of each of these development stages, a usability study or formative evaluation will be performed to evaluate the portion of the course that has just been designed and developed, e.g., course navigation. Analysis of the results of the formative evaluation provides input to the design stage of the next prototype.

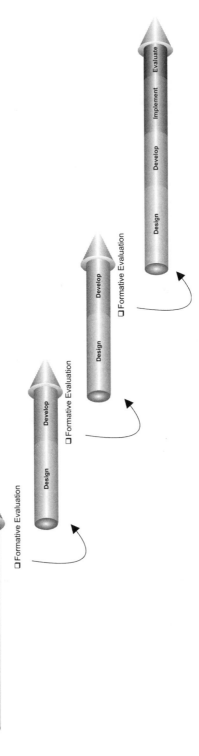

Figure 9.11 Iterative ADDIE course development overview.

Each prototype serves a specific design and development purpose. For example, one prototype might be to create templates for course modules, whereas another may be to test course navigation, assessment techniques, techniques for remote communication, or any other unique portion of the learning experience. The key is identifying appropriate evaluations that will yield the information you need to move forward on development and implementation.

Techniques to perform the formative evaluation might include:

- a survey (questionnaire), possibly administered over the Internet or sent as an e-mail attachment;
- an observation form administered in person;
- a focus group with specific questions asked following the testing; or
- free notes gathered in a word processor and delivered via e-mail.

When all evaluations have been collected, analysis of those evaluations is performed to determine the result (e.g., course navigation is poor and needs to be redesigned, course module 1 did not meet its terminal objectives and needs to be redesigned, course module 2 met all terminal objectives – proceed to the design and development of module 3, etc.). These results are the input to the next design-development stage of the evolutionary design.

The cycle of design-develop-formative evaluation continues until the whole course is developed and evaluated. The WBS for this ADDIE process is a bit different from the processes we have discussed thus far. Let's look at the network diagram for this process first (see Figure 9.12).

As you can see from this diagram, we have inserted four new processes to the previous network diagram. These processes are:

- design iterations – design the iterations (e.g., the first iteration will evaluate course navigation, the second will evaluate potential exercise techniques, etc.);
- iteration 1 – design, develop, develop/install necessary infrastructure and software, implement the iteration, and evaluate the iteration;
- iteration 2 – same as iteration 1 but for a different aspect of the course;
- iteration n – same as iteration 2 but for a different aspect of the course;
- develop the final course – this might be a simple integration of the iteration sections.

Figure 9.13 illustrates the WBS for this iterative course development process. This figure illustrates the relationship of the iterations and the summary tasks contained within each iteration. Note how each iteration also serves as a summary task, with the design, develop, infrastructure, and conduct subtasks duration rolling up to calculate the time period for each iteration.

The recommended deliverables for the iteration cycles are illustrated as

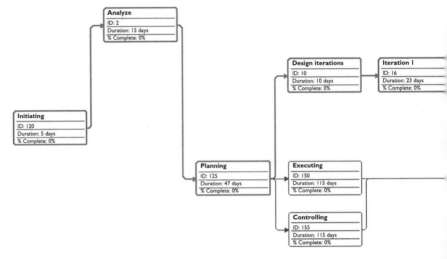

Figure 9.12 Iterative course development network diagram.

activities in Figure 9.14. Only one iteration cycle has been expanded in this figure along with the planning stage for all iterations (see task IDs 10 through 32 of Figure 9.14).

Activities for iteration 2 and iteration 3, task IDs 33 and 50, are similar to those for iteration 1. Thus we have not expanded those sections of the project schedule. Additionally, all the following processes to develop final course, implement the course, and evaluate the course (task IDs 67, 94, and 110) are similar to the non-iterative WBS described earlier in this chapter. Again, this entire project plan has been included on the website for this text (http://www.routledge.com/textbooks/9780415772204) to give you a starting point if you choose to use a desktop scheduling program to plan and schedule your project.

In conclusion

In this chapter we have integrated the separate processes of ADDIE and IPECC discussed in Chapters 2 through 8 into one process. We have developed a WBS that may be used as a starting point for you as you develop a new course, whether you use an iterative or non-iterative ADDIE process. On the website for this text (http://www.routledge.com/textbooks/9780415772204), we have provided two project schedules that may be used as templates for the development of an iterative or non-iterative course WBS.

To use the templates, open the plan using your desktop scheduling application, delete any activities that you do not plan to perform, add activities that are required for your project, and save the schedule. Then open the schedule and update the tasks by modifying the task durations and adding resources. We trust that you will find these templates valuable!

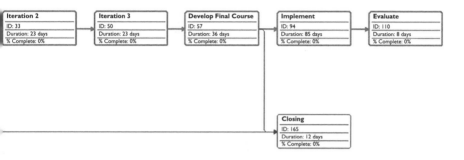

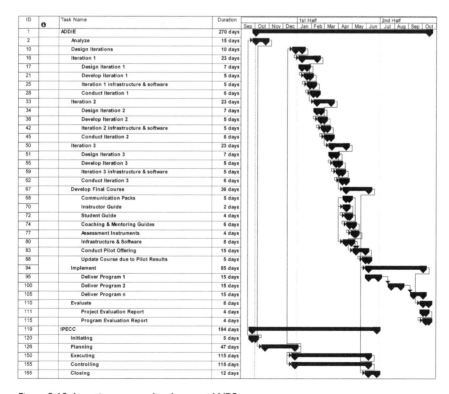

Figure 9.13 Iterative course development WBS.

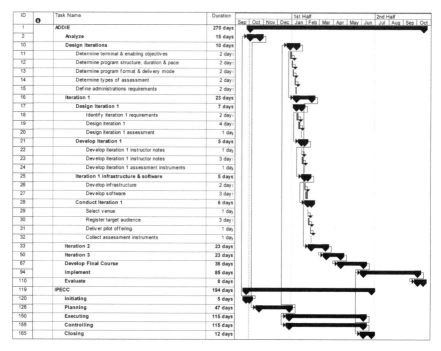

ID	❶	Task Name	Duration
1		ADDIE	270 days
2		Analyze	15 days
10		Design Iterations	10 days
11		Determine terminal & enabling objectives	2 days
12		Determine program structure, duration & pace	2 days
13		Determine program format & delivery mode	2 days
14		Determine types of assessment	2 days
15		Define administrations requirements	2 days
16		Iteration 1	23 days
17		Design Iteration 1	7 days
18		Identify iteration 1 requirements	2 days
19		Design iteration 1	4 days
20		Design iteration 1 assessment	1 day
21		Develop Iteration 1	5 days
22		Develop iteration 1 instructor notes	1 day
23		Develop iteration 1 instructor notes	3 days
24		Develop iteration 1 assessment instruments	1 day
25		Iteration 1 infrastructure & software	5 days
26		Develop infrastructure	2 days
27		Develop software	3 days
28		Conduct Iteration 1	6 days
29		Select venue	1 day
30		Register target audience	3 days
31		Deliver pilot offering	1 day
32		Collect assessment instruments	1 day
33		Iteration 2	23 days
50		Iteration 3	23 days
67		Develop Final Course	36 days
94		Implement	85 days
110		Evaluate	8 days
119		IPECC	194 days
120		Initiating	5 days
126		Planning	47 days
150		Executing	115 days
155		Controlling	115 days
165		Closing	12 days

Figure 9.14 Sample iteration cycle WBS.

Chapter 10

The future of e-learning and its impact on project management

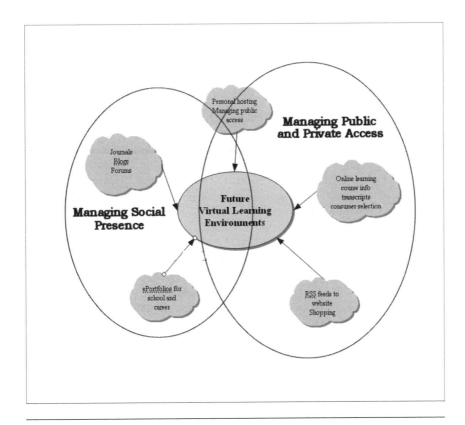

Contrary to popular belief, e-learning environments have been available since the 1960s, though they were not called that. However, the "e" in electronic has been providing learning for nearly 60 years. This type of e-learning was implemented primarily in large corporations. It took the form of text-based training on large mainframe systems, some shared video or point-to-point video conferencing, and even TV broadcasts.

It wasn't until approximately 15 years ago, with the advent of individual computing and shared networks, that e-learning became more readily available and began to be adopted by larger academic institutions. Only during the last five to seven years has e-learning become an important focus for many educational and training organizations, from medium and large corporations to all sizes of colleges and universities. Even the K-12 environment has embraced e-learning to supplement classroom-based instruction or, in the case of home-schooled children, it is sometimes the only form of instruction.

Proponents of e-learning have made many claims to justify the investment – cost savings, just-in-time learning availability, flexible learning styles, etc. These are all good reasons for e-learning and, if we believed all of these claims, the future looks bright indeed. Despite this, only a small percentage of learners (research indicates approximately 10 percent of all learners), both in industry and academia, are using e-learning environments. However, it is on the rise and expanding very rapidly.

Predicting the future

Attempting to predict the future is always difficult. The field of instructional design is strewn with examples of technology with great promise that lasted only a short time. Those who have been around 40 years or so remember the promise of film strips, instructional television, the Laser disk, and the Phillips CDVideo. Each of these were revolutionary and had great ideals behind their design and implementation, but thier tenure was brief. Probably the one lasting system today is instructional television. Though it is no longer (or rarely) used in formal education or training, it is still used extensively to teach those at home through cable access. Of course, the king of all instructional television – *Sesame Street* – still survives today.

Defining what constitutes future technology is also difficult. Instructional technologists tend to label something as new or future technology whenever it comes into their purview, when in reality it may have been available for several years already. Table 10.1 identifies a number of technologies that are now popular, and to some seem very new, but have been around for five years or more.

With a list such as that in Table 10.1, one might ask: "Is the future already here?" Certainly this list gives us a sense that the innovation is created and the technology is available years in advance of its popularity. The question is which of these already useful technologies will survive another decade?

The E-Learning Guild, with a membership of 20,000, regularly commissions research to determine how their members are using e-learning and what their plans are for the future. The results of their 2006 report are recorded in "% of Usage" in Table 10.1. We would hypothesize that those with little usage are likely to disappear and those with high usage are likely to stay over the next decade.

SMS, Instant Messaging, Wikis, and blogs are the loosers in this survey. When looking further at the pedagogy of using these technologies, we find that each of these has an inherent problem or the functionality is already available through a better means of distribution. For example, instant messaging is rarely used in education and training environments. When two or more people want instant communication, they rely on Web-conferencing instead – a medium that provides a more rich environment than text messaging. Blogs are much too egocentric to meet most educational needs. It really is the electronic equivalent

Table 10.1 Technologies and their use

Technology	Introduced	% of Usage
RSS (really simple syndication)	2002	81
Instant messaging	1996	24
Wikis and blogs	1995	15
Embedded performance support	1994	100
Discussion forums	1994	79
Web-conferencing	1994	79
Search tools	1994	100
SMS (short message service)	1992	13
Mobile learning	1991	73
Knowledge management/sharing	1983	94
Audio podcasts	1980	73

of journaling – which is one-way communication. As education moves even more toward high interaction, blogs are seen as a throwback to lectures and single-source knowledge bases. Wikis were cited by the members as too complex to use. If the interface improved, perhaps this tool would be seen as more useful in the future. However, once a tool gets a reputation of being complex, it is very difficult to get back in front of users who have moved on to the next killer application.

What are the delivery trends in the next 5 years?

Three key concepts seem clear in the 2006 study, both formal education students and corporate training attendees want the same things:

1   *Freedom to learn at a time that is convenient.* People want to learn at different times and for different reasons. Those who have grown up with technology already know about virtual classrooms. They now want e-learning via mobile offices they can download and interact with anywhere in the world and at any time of day or night.
2   *Personal choice.* Learners want to make choices at the module level instead of the course level. Too often all the topics in a course are not interesting or needed at that particular time in the learner's life. Embedded e-learning or just-in-time learning as part of the daily job is seen as highly requested. In fact, many students see this type of learning as short bursts of useful information, not "learning."
3   *Peer support in learning.* Though students complain about synchronous activities and group projects, they also do not want to learn on their own. Learners want contact with their peers. They want to discuss and interact and gain knowledge from other people's experiences. However, they want it on their terms. Some corporations are taking advantage of this by using

older or retired individuals as e-tutors in short virtual classrooms. These e-tutors facilitate learning in short bursts ranging from a formal module to a human expert-system. It is a way to save the corporate memory and expertise while providing on-going training for new employees or less experienced employees.

Trends 10 and 15 years away

We need to begin planning for increased e-learning capacity and scalability beyond what we can currently conceive. Trends currently suggest that growth of demand for e-learning from users will grow faster than our supply capability or innovation capacity. Learners will want and demand better and more interactive forms of e-learning, often becoming frustrated by what is not yet available.

The first indication that technology is part of the mainstream of learning will come when the "e" in e-learning disappears. The "e" is a temporary device to talk about the changes in learning we are developing and accessing as the Internet becomes ubiquitous. As learning becomes more integrated with technology, it will be assumed that all learning has electronic access included. It will not be differentiated.

Both in the corporate arena and higher education, digital collaboration will become the norm. Already software companies are finding ways to integrate collaboration with organizational desktops and browsers. Just as every worker has a telephone, every worker will have the ability to add a virtual classroom or meeting space to any telephone call or online conversation.

Instead of students registering for single classes or training events, they will more likely subscribe to "continuous learning" – paying a retainer for learning services that include content delivery and performance support. As part of this learning subscription, learners will be part of an on-going community of learning and practice where expert peers become just as important as expert teachers and trainers.

Higher education institutions will continue to be the major providers of e-learning – particularly if they can adapt to the new model of continuous and just-in-time learning options. Degree programs will not have an end-point; instead they will provide access to lifelong learning communities and feeds from these institutions. Already many higher education institutions are providing perpetual Internet access to alumni. It is only one more step to offer these learning communities and to lead the way in the subscription-based environment.

Simulations will evolve to our expectation level. We will become used to making major decisions by running simulations and debriefing them – in effect trying it out before we invest significant time and resources. Simulations will have multiplayer, on-going, deeply visual capabilities. In addition the web will increase the frequency with which it integrates with the physical world, through simulation. For example, in nursing and medical education, already simulation labs with programmable mannequins access large databases of scenarios and expert feedback for practice prior to engaging with humans.

With the advent of mobile technologies, learning will become device agnostic. Old technologies like phones will find renewed roles in e-learning as they provide mobility. Newer technologies like laptops and handheld computers will increase access to video and audio streams, as well as other ubiquitous learning options. Finally, new equipment will provide Internet access for learning embedded within the hardware.

What is certain is that learning is now engaged in a symbiotic relationship with technology. We will see steady increases in the use of technology for development, delivery, management, and marketing of learning. We will see new models of what a learning experience is like, when linked with the power of technology. We will see technology and learning integrated with daily business tasks and woven into our lives. However, we will not see technology alone. We will continue to see classrooms, with instructors, engaged with technology as well as some learning opportunities that are completely online.

All of these changes will take on an even faster rate of change. In addition to changing delivery methods, institutions will continue to deal with changing roles and careers for learning professionals. Student needs and demands will drive innovation, but so will teachers' creativity push the limits of technology. So, strap on your seat belts. The learning ride will be interesting and powerful.

References

Gitlow, H. and Gitlow, S. (1989). A comparison of the Japanese school of quality and the Deming school of quality. Monograph. University of Miami Institute for the Study of Quality in Manufacturing and Service, Coral Gables, Florida.

Harrington, H. J. (1991). *Business Process Improvement: The Breakthrough Strategy for Total Quality, Productivity, and Competitiveness.* New York: McGraw-Hill.

Horton, W. (2001). *Evaluating E-Learning.* Alexandria, Virginia: American Society for Training & Development.

Jones, J., Aguirre, D. and Calderone, M. (2004, Summer). 10 principles of change management. *Strategies – Business Journal,* 35.

Juran, J. (1988). *Juran's Quality Control Handbook.* 4th edn. New York: McGraw-Hill.

Kancheva, E. (2002). *Key Considerations for Successful Outsourcing of IT Functions in Higher Education.* Educause Center for Applied Research, Research Bulletin, Volume 2002, Issue 13, July 25.

Kirkpatrick, D. (1998). *Evaluating Training Programs.* San Francisco: Berrett-Koehler Publishers.

Kolas, L. and Staupe, A. (2006, Jan–March). Implementing delivery methods by using pedagogical design patterns. *Journal of Distance Education Technologies,* 4(1), 56–70.

Project Management Institute (2004). *A Guide to the Project Management Body of Knowledge (PMBOK® Guide).* 3rd edn. Atlanta, GA.

Glossary of terms

Whenever a book is filled with processes and new concepts there tends to be a plethora of terminology introduced and used throughout the text. To make matters even more challenging to someone new to this field, the definitions of these terms tend to change with whatever is the new marketing buzz for that year. The glossary presented here represents the author's implied meaning when using these terms throughout the text. Most of the definitions are what we believe to be the most accepted definition in the fields of E-learning, Instructional Design, and Project Management. Where a definition was not clearly delineated in the field, we substituted our own best understanding of the concept.

aim The stated high-level summary of the project's objectives.

assumption A statement that is taken as being true for the purposes of planning a project, but which could change later. An assumption is made where some facts are not yet known or decided and is usually reserved for matters of such significance that if they change or turn out not to be true then the project will need considerable replanning.

Examples of assumptions include: funding will be made available as part of the legislative budget for education; or we will not need to procure hosting services.

baseline A snapshot. A position or situation that is recorded with the specific intention of using it to compare against some future position, usually to demonstrate that change has been achieved.

In planning, a baseline captures when the activities within the plan were originally intended to occur. When a plan is baselined, the currently planned start and finish dates of all tasks within the plan are separately recorded. If the plan is subsequently updated with any changes to these dates, any slippage can be measured against the originally planned (baseline) dates. A plan is normally baselined once it has been signed off by the project board.

The term baseline is also used in evaluation similarly to describe the position against which future measurements can be compared.

benefit   A positive outcome of a project or program.

The process of "benefit tracking" is one of ensuring that, as the project progresses, the expected benefits are being delivered.

The term outcome can be used to include benefits.

business case   A business case documents the justification for the undertaking of a project based on the estimated cost of development and the anticipated benefits to be gained.

It secures senior management and stakeholder commitment from the outset. It is also the vehicle by which the sponsor and project board confirm and accept the foundation for a project, prior to the commencement of work and the agreement of resources. It is the case by which the ongoing viability of the project is monitored and will provide a basis for the project closure report and the post-implementation review.

change control   The process, whether simple or complex, by which suggested changes to a project's scope, plan, or deliverables can be recorded, managed, and controlled. Uncontrolled changes to scope or plans are one of the most common causes of failure in projects, usually because these lead either to the wrong things being delivered or to the project having insufficient resources to deliver the changed (and usually increased) scope. Change control should not be confused with change management.

change management   The processes by which the actions required to make change happen, either within an organization or to external stakeholders or the environment in which they operate, can be managed. Change management is typically a cross-cutting activity and may concern changes to people or their behavior as well as to the institution's processes, organizational structures, or technology. Most Projects are concerned with implementing change of some description and therefore change management is an important element of them.

change request   A submission to change the scope or plan of a project or the quality of one of its deliverables. When using a formal project management methodology these are usually recorded in a physical document. Change requests normally form part of the change control process, but it is possible to have procedures that do not require the completion of physical documents to process and manage change requests.

checkpoint   A meeting held at regular, and usually frequent, intervals between the project manager and the project team to review the progress of a project.

constraint   Something which is mandated, unavoidable, or which may prevent the project manager from delivering the project in the most appropriate way, and which cannot be changed. A constraint restricts the possible ways of approaching the project.

Examples are:

• Delivery of the project or a particular outcome may be mandatory on a certain date (for example the work which was required to ensure year 2000 compliance).

- The project approach may mandate the use of specific standards, processes, legislative practices, or particular ways of working (for example the need to comply with SCORM standards in selecting and migrating to a learning object repository).

Constraints should be documented at the start of a project to ensure that all those involved are aware of any pre-set parameters. It also provides an opportunity for stakeholders to comment on the validity of each constraint and possibly provide the project manager with additional room for maneuvering. Constraints are usually considered alongside assumptions and the two are often confused.

contingency plan   Used in risk management, this is a series of activities you plan in advance to reduce or eliminate the impact of a risk AFTER it has occurred. Sometimes referred to as a fallback plan.

critical network chart   A term sometimes used to describe a milestone chart.

critical path   The set of deliverables which, when carried out sequentially, together determine the overall timescale of a project (that is – if any one of them takes longer than planned then the whole project will take that much longer). To determine the critical path requires full knowledge of task durations, dependencies, and resources.

This term is very often misinterpreted to mean those tasks that it is believed are most important to a project's success – it is important to realize that the true critical path may change over time and may sometimes encompass activities which were originally thought to be unimportant. Understanding the critical path is useful in the prioritizing effort and resources.

critical success factor (CSF)   Something that must be in place for a Project to deliver its benefits or outcomes. A critical success factor is often what makes the difference between just delivering something and really making a difference.

CSFs are internal or external factors that the organization undertaking the project can control or strongly influence. In a project context they are generally more about culture than about what must be done or delivered. Analysis of critical success factors will generate activities that should be undertaken to ensure the conditions are in place for success (for example a communications strategy to explain the benefits of doing things differently or development of a training plan).

cross-cutting   An issue or project is described as cross-cutting where it affects a large number of areas of work within an organization. This is distinct from a dependency which is between two or more small number of areas of work. Typically cross-cutting issues include change management, communications, knowledge management, training, and perhaps IT developments.

deliverable   Something you produce or deliver during a project in order to achieve one or more objectives. Deliverables do NOT necessarily have to be physical things like documents. Some examples could be:

- a learning management system or learning object repository;
- a set of guidance notes;
- a Project team.

Each deliverable should be linked to at least one project objective (otherwise why are you producing it?).

Planning is normally carried out by a logical process of working out what deliverables you need to produce and then working out what activities you need to carry out to produce them.

Deliverables are often confused with objectives – essentially, a deliverable, or set of deliverables, is what you produce to achieve the objective.

dependency   Within a project, a relationship which indicates that the starts or ends of two separate tasks on a project plan are linked together.

Within a project, a dependency is usually a deliverable from one project which another project needs in order for it to make progress.

escalation   The process of raising the profile of a risk or issue to a higher level in a project hierarchy, usually because it is not possible to deal with it at the level at which it was originally recorded.

Some examples of this include:

- The resources required to carry out the management actions to deal with the risk or issue cannot be found within the project team.
- Project issue has remained unresolved to the point where its impact becomes so severe that it could affect the delivery of a project goal or objective.

evaluation   A series of activities you carry out to ascertain whether a project has achieved its goal. Often evaluation activities are left until the end of a project, but they should generally be planned in from the start. This avoids the problem, for instance, of having no baseline against which to evaluate the project.

fallback plan   See contingency plan.

Gantt chart   A pictorial representation of a project plan, showing deliverables (usually as shaded bars); milestones (usually as black diamonds); and dependencies (usually as lines linking the relevant ends of the activity bars).

The word GANTT is often capitalized and is often assumed to be an acronym but is in fact the name of the man who invented the technique (Henry Gantt, American pioneer in the field of scientific approaches to management).

goal   See outcome.

impact   In risk and issue management – the degree to which a risk or an issue will affect a project's ability to deliver its objectives.

Impact is usually rated subjectively on a scale of high-medium-low. It is important to realize that the impact may need to be reassessed if the risk or issue is escalated to a higher level in the project hierarchy – what may seem a high impact to an individual project may well be of significantly lesser impact when rated against other project objectives.

interdependency   A shorthand way to define a two-way dependency at a high level.

At this level they are not manageable other than by treating them as risks, constraints, or Assumptions. To be managed effectively they must be broken down into their constituent low-level dependencies within the relevant project plans.

issue   An unresolved question, a requirement to modify or change a project deliverable, or a problem which has already arisen, or which it is known is certain to arise, which will impact on a project's ability to deliver one or more of its objectives.

There is commonly a great deal of confusion between issues and risks.

However, it is more important to decide whether the problem needs to be managed and, if so, what action needs to be taken, than it is to spend too much time debating whether it is a risk or an issue.

issue register   A document used to record the issues facing a project, usually set out as a table in either Word or Excel. It should, as a minimum, record a description of each issue, an assessment of the impact and the action to be taken to address it, though it can be more sophisticated.

knowledge management   The explicit management of Project-related information within a project. Knowledge, in this context, is interpreted as anything that someone else might find useful. It can therefore consist of:

- best practices;
- guidance letters or memos;
- exemplary material examples or templates;
- reports;
- rules of thumb, and so on.

likelihood   See probability.

management actions   In risk management – a term used collectively to describe the counter-measures and contingency plans which are defined or put in place to manage the probability or impact of a risk in issue management – the actions which are being or will be taken to manage the impact of an issue.

methodology   When applied to project management, a set of pre-defined tools and techniques which can be followed as part of a standard management process. Good methodologies are based on a wealth of distilled experience and can be useful as a point of reference. However methodologies should be used appropriately – they are not of themselves a guarantee of success. The IPECC methodology was the foundation of this book.

Microsoft Project   One example of a software tool which can be used to support the production and maintenance of project plans. It is mostly used just to produce Gantt charts and work breakdown structures, but can be very much more sophisticated when used to its full extent.

milestone   A point at which you can measure progress on the way to achieving an objective. Sometimes used interchangeably to show on a plan the production or completion of a deliverable, or the meeting of an objective.

Milestones are usually phrased using the name of the relevant Deliverable, activity, or objective followed by a passive verb, for example: "submission agreed," "website launched," or "project team in place" to identify that the milestone has been achieved.

milestone chart   A chart showing key Milestones for a project which is used by the project manager to monitor progress.

objective   Something you need to achieve in order to meet your aim. To be effective, objectives should always be written so that they are SMART (Specific, Measurable, Achievable, Relevant, Time-bound). The project should produce at least one deliverable in support of each objective (otherwise, how are you going to achieve it?).

outcome   A resulting effect (whether positive or negative) of carrying out a project. A positive outcome is usually referred to as a benefit.

output   See deliverable.

phase   See stage.

probability   In risk management – how probable it is that a risk will actually happen. This can be rated on a high (very probable) – medium (likely) – low (unlikely but possible) scale, but can be much more sophisticated. Probability does not change when risks are escalated.

product   See deliverable.

project   A related group of work activities organized at the direction of a project manager using a set of project plans which, when carried out, achieve a certain aim or set of objectives. It is important to understand that a project is something that can be planned and is something with a specific end in sight and which is managed to deliver as a single coherent whole.

Projects should therefore not be confused with reactive or "business as usual" activities.

A project normally has the following typical attributes:

- specific budget;
- defined start and end dates;
- specifically allocated resources with clearly defined roles;

- specific objectives and deliverables;
- processes for managing risks, issues, and dependencies and controlling changes.

project board   The set of individuals who collectively monitor and control a project's overall progress and act as a quality assurance mechanism for its deliverables and an escalation (and resolution) route for risks and issues.

A true project board typically consists of no more than about six people and concentrates almost entirely on the process of project management. The term project board can be a much-abused and confused concept. It is often used to encompass a large group of people who merely have an interest in a project or who it is felt need to be consulted or kept on board.

This is NOT a project board – it is a stakeholder group. It is also sometimes used to describe a group whose members focus on strategic direction of the project rather than the process of project management – this is a steering group. It is possible for a project board to fulfill the functions of a steering group or a stakeholder group, but this should never be at the expense of its project management role.

project charter   A document produced at the start of a project to define what it is doing, for the purposes of agreement by the project board. Also sometimes referred to as a project brief or a project initiation document (PID).

A typical project charter will include:

- definitions of a project's rationale (or business case);
- goal and objectives;
- scope;
- success criteria;
- deliverables;
- major activities (usually as phases and stages);
- timescales;
- organization and management arrangements;
- initial assessment of key risks, issues, constraints, assumptions, and critical success factors;
- approaches to project management processes such as risk and issue management.

project manager   The person who has overall day-to-day control of a project and is responsible for ensuring it is delivered.

project plan   The "route map" showing how a project will achieve its objectives by producing its deliverables, and meeting its milestones. Often the terms project plan and Gantt chart are used interchangeably but a true Project plan is more than just a Gantt chart.

It should also encompass information about:

- the resources allocated to specific tasks;
- the links between activities and the objectives; and
- the dependencies between the tasks and the deliverables.

The term "project plan" is sometimes confused with project charter although the two are very different. One of the most common things inexperienced project managers do is to develop a project plan and then ignore it (thinking they have "done" project planning. There is little point investing time and effort in developing a plan if you are not intending to use it actively to manage your work. The plan needs to be maintained regularly to reflect actual progress which will provide information for progress monitoring, highlight problems arising from slippage, and act as a tool for reprioritizing work.

project sponsor   The person who is accountable for the successful delivery of a project, who usually has control over the resources allocated to it, and to whom the project manager reports progress and escalates issues for resolution.

quality   The collection of features and characteristics of a deliverable or service that define its ability to satisfy the stated or implied needs of the customer who commissioned it. Quality is therefore the standards and criteria to which the project's deliverables must be delivered for them to perform effectively. The deliverable must provide the functions expected, and solve the problem for which it was created. It must deliver the benefit and value expected of it.

It must also meet other performance requirements, or service levels, such as availability, reliability, and maintainability, and have acceptable levels of finish and polish. The way that quality will be managed should be described within a project's quality plan.

quality assurance   The processes that are put in place to demonstrate that deliverables are of sufficient quality. Quality assurance and quality control are very similar and often used interchangeably. Strictly speaking, quality assurance is used to describe the process by which quality can be demonstrated to have been achieved, whereas quality control is about the processes to be put in place to achieve that quality.

quality control (QC)   The processes put in place to ensure that deliverables are of sufficient quality. Quality assurance and quality control are very similar and often used interchangeably. Strictly speaking quality assurance is used to describe the process by which quality can be demonstrated to have been achieved, whereas quality control is about the processes to be put in place to achieve that quality.

quality management plan   Part of a project plan which describes how quality will be achieved. It can describe both quality control and quality assurance processes.

requirements definition   A requirement is a description of what a system should do. Systems may have from dozens to thousands of requirements. E-learning systems may have multiple levels of requirements definitions (e.g., course requirements, staff skill requirements, evaluation requirements, etc.).

resource   In project management terms, something which enables a task on a project plan to be carried out. Usually this refers to people, but could also be money or materials.

risk   A situation which may occur in the future and which, if it were to occur, could impact on the ability of a project to deliver one or more of its goals or objectives.

When considering risks you should think about what may stop you from achieving the aim/outcome(s) of the project as well as the extent to which critical success factors (CSFs) are in place that will ensure success. Risks are normally recorded on a risk register.

risk register   A document used to record the risks facing a project, usually produced as a table in either Word or Excel. It should, as a minimum, record a description of each risk, an assessment of its severity and the action to be taken to minimize the risk, though it can be more sophisticated.

scope   The "boundary" within which a project is planned and managed. Can be thought of as having five "dimensions":

- logical – the processes within the organization which are affected;
- organizational – who is affected by the project;
- deliverable – what will be delivered and (sometimes crucially) what will not;
- temporal – the time "window" during which the project must be carried out or which affects when particular activities can or cannot be undertaken; and
- financial – what are the budgetary constraints.

When defining the scope of a project it is equally as important to consider what is outside the project's scope as it is to define what is within it. Doing this makes it clear what the project manager is NOT responsible for delivering. If this boundary should change then the change control process should be invoked. A clear boundary makes it much easier to know when this must happen.

scope creep   The process by which the set of deliverables which a project is producing changes over time, usually in an uncontrolled fashion and almost always increasing rather than decreasing, without a consequent change in resources or review of the deliverability of the project. Uncontrolled scope creep is one of the most common causes of project failure.

severity   In risk management, an overall indicator of the significance of a risk (where one is required), usually calculated on the basis of a combination of the impact and probability of the risk. Severity is usually rated on a scale of high-medium-low for simplicity, but can also be ascribed an actual numeric value to enable risks to be ranked in priority order. Care should be taken to include a key where numeric values are used (i.e., does 1 = lowest or highest priority?).

sign-off   The formal agreement that confirms a deliverable is fit for purpose. Sign-off can be achieved either by correspondence (or e-mail) or at designated sign-off meetings (which may form part of a project board meeting). It is important for sign-off to be formally recorded in some way.

Sometimes sign-off can be achieved quite simply (for example through the use of meeting minutes). However, for key deliverables it may be appropriate to ask reviewers physically to sign a document to indicate their acceptance. Note that project management deliverables such as the project charter should also be signed off.

It is good practice to agree to sign-off arrangements at the start of the activity which leads to the production of a deliverable, so that sign-off can be properly incorporated into the project plan.

sponsor   A person in a senior position within the organization who supports (and is seen to support) the aim or outcome of a project. This sponsorship should legitimize the work of the project.

The sponsor must be in a sufficiently senior position in the organization to influence the allocation of resources and commitment of time to the project by other senior staff. The role of sponsor is usually filled by an executive, but other senior staff can also sponsor the project. Furthermore, in the case of e-learning projects that are a single course or a few related courses, the sponsor may be a senior faculty member, a dean, or a curriculum committee rather than an executive.

stage   The highest level grouping of work shown on a project plan. Throughout this text we used the stages of ADDIE to define these levels. Also called phases, where we used the phases of IPECC to define high-level groupings as well.

stakeholder   Any person or organization having an interest in the progress or outcomes of a project – usually because they are either part of it or affected by what it delivers.

The process of working out which stakeholders are most and least important to successful project delivery is called stakeholder analysis and the processes by which input from, and communications with, them are collectively controlled is called stakeholder management.

stakeholder group   A group comprising selected stakeholders and project staff, and which is constituted to advise a project board from a stakeholder perspective. The creation of a stakeholder group can be useful in gaining both stakeholder buy-in as well as providing ideas on how to implement a project successfully.

Stakeholder groups are often a vital part of successful change management. A stakeholder group acts purely in an advisory capacity and has no executive power within the project or power to change the strategy.

steering group   A group, normally comprised of the organization's senior managers, who set the strategic direction of a project. A steering group does not usually involve itself in monitoring progress, except to the extent required to fulfill its function – this is left to the project board. The steering group may sometimes also involve key stakeholders, but a separate stakeholder group may be considered more appropriate.

step   This is not really a traditional project management term, but can be used to denote an interim milestone on the way to achieving an outcome.

steps and outcomes chart   A term which can be used for a milestone chart showing key project milestones and outcomes.

success criteria   The criteria by which a Project will be measured in order to determine whether it has been successful. Also sometimes described as a target. Success criteria should not be confused with critical success factors (CSFs).

success factor   See critical success factor.

target   Something you are aiming for – usually the numerically measurable part of an objective.

task   The lowest level of work shown on a project plan. Some examples could include:

- write draft report;
- review first draft; and
- modify report.

In an ideal project plan, a task is allocated to a single individual and should last no more than a few days. As in the above examples, tasks are usually defined using a phrase or sentence beginning with an active verb followed by a noun.

vision   The vision is a description of what the world will be like as a result of the project and seeks to define the desired outcomes. The vision statement should form the basis for all work on a project and will inevitably evolve over the life of the project.

Index